INTERLUDE
IN
UMBARGER

INTERLUDE IN UMBARGER

Italian POWs and a Texas Church

Donald Mace Williams

TEXAS TECH UNIVERSITY PRESS

This book was set in 12 on 16 ITC Baskerville and printed on acid-
free paper that meets the guidelines for permanence and
durability of the Committee on Production Guidelines for Book
Longevity of the Council on Library Resources.

Cover art linocut of the Hereford P.O.W. camp by Dino Gambetti
Jacket and book design by Kelley Ferguson Farwell

Manufactured in the United States of America

Library of Congress Cataloging-in-Publication Data
Williams, Donald Mace.
    Interlude in Umbarger: Italian POWs and a Texas Church /by
Donald Mace Williams.
        p.   cm.
    Includes bibliographical references.
    ISBN 0-89672-276-7 (cloth)
    1. World War, 1939-1945—Prisoners and prisons, American.
    2. Hereford Military Reservation and Reception Center (Tex.)-
-History. 3. St. Mary's Church (Umbarger, Tex.) 4. Hereford
(Tex.)—History. 5. Umbarger (Tex.)—History. 6. Di Bello , Franco.
7. Prisoners of war—Italy—Biography. 8. Prisoners of war—United
States—Biography. I. Title.
D805.U5W55 1992
940.54'7273'092245—dc20   91-43641
                                                               CIP

Texas Tech University Press
Lubbock, Texas 79409-1037 USA

92 93 94 95 96 97 98 99 / 9 8 7 6 5 4 3 2 1

Acknowledgments

When I first heard about the Italian prisoners of war who had executed the works of art in St. Mary's Church at Umbarger, Texas, I was working for the *Amarillo Globe-News*, and I took a journalist's pleasure in the story. It was a dozen years before I decided to look further into the episode, but I still approached it as a feature story, looking first for sources to interview and second for documents. As it developed, military records and diocesan files provided vital information that interviews could never have brought out. I have listed sources of such documents elsewhere and have referred to them in footnotes. Here I want to acknowledge with gratitude the many people, including present and former residents of Umbarger, former prisoners of war at the Hereford camp, former military and civilian employees of the camp, men and women of the cloth, Panhandle farmers, and others, who took the time to give me (in interviews and by correspondence) the information that forms much of the skeleton and nearly all the spirit of this account.

Foremost among these is Franco Di Bello, who forty-five years ago was one of the three painters of the St. Mary's works. His recollections, enriched by the diary he kept while he was a prisoner, are the source of the main body of this story. He wrote dozens of long letters to me in his fluent English, and he not only loaded me with reminiscences during a week of interviews at his apartment in Pordenone but also drove me across much of northern Italy for interviews with other *herefordiani*—interviews for which he was the highly competent interpreter. I owe him my deepest gratitude.

John Coyle, with the same generosity that melted the hostilities of the crew of artists he nominally guarded, gave up many hours to talks and correspondence with me about the project and the Hereford camp. About Umbarger and St. Mary's Church during the time of the project, my best source was Jerry Skarke Gerber, who found time amid an unremittingly busy life to give me many indispensable recollections. I am warmly grateful to both.

I owe thanks also to Louise Alfano, Barbara Anderson, Harvey Artho, Joe Artho, Kenneth Artho, Leo Artho, Ormalene Artho, Theresa Artho, Marie Barnard, Elsie Batenhorst, Mrs. Charles Beckman, Clarence Beckman, the Reverend Arnold A. Boeding, Armando Boscolo, Archie M. Bottoms, Amalia Bracht, Alessandro Brighenti, George Brockman, Mary Brockman, Alberto Burri, Joseph R. Carvolth, Jr., Kenneth H. Clausen, Ann Payton Connelly, Grace Covington, Dixie Cox, Evelyn Coyle, Clara de Cristofaro, Blanche Cross,

Reeves Donnell, Sister Martina Eiber, Rose Evers,
Pauline Farmer, Sister Charles Marie Foster, Joe
Frank, Vincent Friemel, Dino Gambetti, Arnold Gavin,
Ann Skarke Gerber, Bernice Gerber, Seletta Gholson,
Giuseppe Giorgi, Mae Grimes, Grant Hanna, Mike
Harter, the Reverend Vincent Heald, Donald Heiney,
Rachel Henslee, Rose Hoffman, Ernie Hollenstein,
Don Houle, Jack T. Hughes, W. P. Janssen, Giulio Job,
Lee Johnson, Emilio Jori, Gustave Kaplan, Anna
Kleman, Esther Klinke, Ben Koch, Helen Koch, Stefan
Kramar, Carol Lindemann, Odessa Lindemann, Holmes
Lovejoy, Aurelio Manzoni, the Right Reverend
Andrew Marthaler, Dominic T. Mastrianni, Phyllis
Mathis, the Most Reverend L. T. Matthiesen, the Right
Reverend Monroe John Matthiesen, Boone McClure,
Leland McMurray, Jim Mercer, Linda Milburn, Luigi
Montalbetti, the Right Reverend Peter Morsch, Ann
Cockrell Osburn, Teresa Evers Parr, Bill Phipps, the
Reverend John Quatannens, Alfredo Rizzon, Joe D.
Rogers, Sister Nellie Rooney, the Reverend James
Salvi, A.J. Schroeter, Helen Skypala, Norbert Skypala,
the Right Reverend Francis Smyer, Mario Springolo,
Gastone Valentinis, Ernesto van Boelhouwer, Benjamin
T. Ware, Jr., Bobby Weaver, Conrad Westhoff, Ed
Wieck, Edna Wieck, Joe Wieck, John Wieck, Viola
Wieck, Carl Wimberly, and Mike Yeary.

I owe gratitude also to R. C. Phelan and to my son,
Andrew M. Williams, for their valuable comments on
an earlier version of the manuscript, and to my wife,
Nell, for her encouragement and help from the beginning of research through the last revision.

The Hereford POW camp in linoleum cut by Dino
Gambetti.

ONE

Partly out of fear of vandalism to the works of art inside, the doors of the church were kept locked until the last few years. The parishioners saw the works on Sundays—and most of them did, and do, attend mass faithfully. Outsiders have seldom gone in; the little town, Umbarger, like all towns in the Texas Panhandle, is pretty well off to itself, and the nearest neighbor, Canyon, has its own small Catholic church. Besides, Umbarger has always been essentially a ring of German-flavored farms looking inward toward the church and not wanting or expecting outsiders, even Catholic ones, to brush past. The priest assigned to St. Mary's at the time the art was put there, which was just at the end of World War II, once approached a family from Amarillo that was visiting for mass and said, "Why don't you go to your own church?"

So the murals, the carvings, and the one big canvas have remained pretty much a private gallery for Umbarger. Even on the weekend every November when hundreds of people from Amarillo and the rest of the Panhandle come to the German-sausage dinner in the parish hall next door, the church has been open only the last year or so. Umbarger people old enough to remember the hollow-eyed Italian prisoners of war who came to the church to work with paint brushes and carving tools are generally hospitable and willing to reminisce about that period. About numerous, sometimes disrespectful visitors, most of them would probably feel as the former priest did.

It is not this book's purpose to decide whether the art itself, if accessible, would have justified many visitors. The art is at least of a quality to make the inside of the church a "totally unexpected" sight in its region, as the inspectors who in the early 1980s nominated St. Mary's for placement on the National Register of Historic Places said in their report.[1] They judged the art outstanding in design and craftsmanship. No doubt they would have been surprised to know that it was completed in forty-one working days.

Outsiders who know about the art are likely to suppose that the artists put it there out of gratitude to their humane captors. Many Umbarger residents, including some who were around at the time, suppose the same. In fact, the prisoners' sentiments about the American officials of the Hereford Military Reservation and Reception Center, where they were held, twenty-six miles to the west, were largely bitter ones in those summer and fall months of 1945 after the end of the war in Europe. The officials generally reciprocated the sentiments.

The seven prisoners who did the art work, like virtually all other prisoners in the camp by that time, were stubborn noncollaborationists who had refused to renounce their vows as fighting men. They were therefore known, with hostility and with some accuracy, as "Mussolini men." Partly as a consequence of their refusal, they had had their rations cut to a level below that necessary for happiness and health, and they were well into the scheming and thieving stages of hunger. Their motives in accepting the Umbarger project, which the priest at St. Mary's had arranged as a way to get talented artists for very little expenditure, had something to do with curiosity and with the chance to be among civilians, including women. But the main attraction was the prospect of a good country meal every noontime in the basement of the church.

After a few days of those meals and of the relaxed air in the church, the captive artists did indeed become friendly with Umbarger people (more than friendly, in at least once instance). Hence the sentimental and wishful memories among the hosts. The Italians did not create the same impression among American soldiers and officers at the prison camp, many of whom thought them obstructionist, destructive, and obnoxious. These prisoners had refused to give up their adherence to a repugnant system, and they had nursed their activist nostalgia for its late leader. As expected of Mediterranean prisoners, furthermore, they protested their treatment in theatrically excessive terms. It is no wonder that the commander of the camp felt tempted to punish them, even to underfeed them. Giving in to the temptation is another matter. The commander never starved any of his prisoners to death, but he cut their rations to an inhumane level. For Americans who suppose that only the enemy mistreats captives, the last months of the POW camp at Hereford are not a prideworthy episode.

During the first two years of the camp, which received its first prisoners in April 1943, food was plentiful (by the prisoners' own accounts) and of good quality. The change came almost immediately after the victory in Europe, when, as a former prisoner relates, the Allies "found a number of those infamous extermination camps where the Nazists had caused the death of millions of people by starvation or directly killing them." This discovery, he surmised, led to the order that brought on the bad times for the Hereford prisoners. As a matter of fact, it was not the order itself, but the misapplication of it by the American command at the Hereford camp, that was to blame. This was the effect, in the words of Franco Di Bello, at the time a second lieutenant in captivity at Hereford:

> In a matter of days, food and all items on sale at the PX [Post Exchange] were cut down to almost nothing and we found ourselves deprived not only of the necessary nourishment, but also of the possibility to exercise any activities. Many of us thought it was not worthy of the Americans acting like that and the new treatment was to be temporary. But it wasn't and things went on that way till we left the U.S. After two or three months of this absurd policy our life in the Camp had become really tough and miserable: people began to fall sick (five of them would have died in the following months), quite a few began to show mental disorders, most of us spent almost

the entire day in bed and many became a prey to distrust and pessimism.

No one in fact died of hunger in the camp;[2] and largely because of the intervention of the Catholic bishop of Amarillo, conditions were somewhat improved before Di Bello and most of the other prisoners left for Italy. Nonetheless, his account was substantially accurate. It was in the midst of the period of bad conditions that the project at St. Mary's Church began. And although the project meant relief for Di Bello and the other six participants, the approximately 3,000 prisoners[3]—especially the 800-odd officers—who did not join them stayed hungry.

This account is concerned mainly with the months starting at the onset of the lean period in May 1945, and it essentially ends with the end of the project at St. Mary's Church, by which time conditions in camp had begun to ease. Because Di Bello was a leader in the church project and is articulate in recounting his days in camp, much of the narration reflects his experiences. He has a further qualification as the central figure in a story about uncooperative prisoners and their treatment: he was a zealous noncollaborationist, taught from childhood to be loyal to Benito Mussolini.

T W O

Franco Di Bello, a schoolteacher's child, spent his early boyhood in villages amid the flat farmlands of northeastern Italy. In Percoto, south of Udine, the two-story gray-stone building where his mother taught downstairs and the family lived upstairs is still standing. So are the chestnut tree he used to climb and the stone wall at the corner of the grounds, onto which he would lift his younger brother Bruno to watch for their mother to come back from marketing. In those days, his father rode a bicycle a bumpy three miles over the gravel roads to Udine, where he was a payroll officer in the army.

Franco Di Bello was one of his mother's pupils for the first three years of his schooling. Disciplined when another child might have been let off, he learned the peril of privilege.

"Once, she left the room—maybe to speak with someone, I don't know," Di Bello said. "We began to shout and horse around. When she came back, I was in the first desk, and she shouted and at the same time slapped me."

"You are the first one. You understand you have to give examples to the others," she told him.

His mother, Ida Mannucci di Bello (the parents did not capitalize the *d*), who came from Tuscany, in the north, was the disciplinarian at home as well as at school. His father, Eugenio, was a sweet-natured, demonstrative South Italian who played the violin and loved opera, an interest not shared by the rest of the family. When his father tuned in an operatic broadcast on the family's floor-model Manieti Marelli radio, Franco escaped to his room. He still dislikes opera, but he has a pleasant baritone voice and likes to sing American popular music of the 1940s.

Ida di Bello made herself an example of discipline. After the family had moved to Udine, when Franco was in the fourth grade, she would get her umbrella and her satchel of books, put on her hat, sedately mount her bicycle, and ride four graveled miles to her teaching job at an elementary school in Pradamano. She did everything in the house on top of her job, even the two boys having no regular chores. She cooked meals her husband's southern way, with tomatoes, peppers, and spices, though that was not her way. (Franco Di Bello, who always has thought himself like her rather than like his father—analytical rather than emotional—developed a possibly tendentious allergy to garlic during his adolescence.) When she was packing her son's clothes for his trip to military school at Rome, she told him, "Remember, Franco, that life is sacrifice, but sacrifice is never sterile." Later he wrote that precept into the abbreviated diary he kept at Hereford.

The di Bellos moved to Udine in 1929, when Franco was nine. In Piazza Vittoria, a child could make a game of hopping from gray tile to pink tile on the floor of the Venetian-style city hall and could watch the two mechanical slaves beat out the half-hours from the top of the clock tower on the Loggia del Lionello on the east side of the piazza. Udine was part of the Republic of Venice for centuries. The influence shows in the public buildings and in the graceful windows of the old houses.

In his school days amid such visible order, Franco learned to love rules and to be serene in punishment. It was a formula well conceived for the production of a future noncollaborator. He saw left-handed students with the forbidden hand tied behind them. Using the standard calligraphy, he wrote reports in the prescribed diction: "Today *il signor maestro* spoke about the *'festa del fiore* . . . .'" He memorized a little notebook's-worth of poems and added the flourish of a neat crayon drawing at the top of each poem. Above the *"Marcia Reale,"* the royal hymn, with the refrain *"Viva il Re!* the joyous trumpets blare" he drew a boy in the uniform of the *Balilla* holding the green, white, and red Italian flag on a staff. The boy wore shorts and, except for his black shirt, looked much like a Boy Scout.

Sports, to Ida di Bello, meant bruised knees, neglected studies, rough talk, worn-out shoes, and dirty shirts. For a time in his early adolescence, she forbade Franco to play soccer, though by then he thought of almost nothing else. A big game was coming up, and Franco packed a suitcase with his shoes, shorts, and jersey; lowered it by a string from his second-floor window; let himself down to a garage roof; and jumped. When he came home from the game that night, he was sentenced to three days in his room under the usual punishment of silence from both parents. Since he thought the punishment just, he did not protest. Today he says that if he should be justly accused of some crime, he would not hire a lawyer to defend him. He would want to be punished.

Whether or not Franco took after his mother as much as he liked to believe, he admired his father enough that from the beginning he was determined to follow him in his career. Eugenio was a proud soldier, though in those days a pencil-pushing administrative officer. He had served as a reserve second lieutenant in combat in the first world war and for a year and a half had been a prisoner in Hungary. He was a broad-shouldered man, a little thick in the middle, hawk-nosed and somewhat taller than the South Italian average. On his bicycle, ready to leave for the barracks, he wore nearly knee-high boots, a cap with a braid, and a broad leather belt. His sword was stuck down from the handlebars along the left side of the front wheel. The Italian army had splendid trappings in those days when Mussolini's epinephrine ran high.

Franco had playmates, but his chief outside interest was *calcio*. If he was alone, he would bounce a soccer ball off the wall for practice. He did not pretend.

"I hadn't that much fantasy," he says. "My plays were mostly sports play." He didn't daydream much about travel and adventure, but he wished he could see America, a new and exciting place by the evidence of books and pictures.

At the discipline of soccer, Franco by the age of fifteen had become an outstanding participant, strong and fast; his coach had talked Ida di Bello into rescinding her order. The coach, Mario Cabai, was the right one to influence her, for he had a conscience like hers. Rules, to him, were moral precepts. In soccer, a player can sometimes get by with shoving an opponent away from the ball unobserved, but Cabai would not hear of his players' trying this. He taught loyalty to oneself and to the ideals of the team. The lessons encouraged Franco to police himself later in life, when he might suddenly stop running in the middle of a game. "I thought I was offside," he would explain.

Franco had his sixth birthday when fascism was four years old, and like practically all Italian boys he became one of the *Figli della lupa,* little Romuluses and Remuses of the Fascist youth program. At school, his teachers taught him obedience to Mussolini. When he was nine, Franco joined the *Balilla,* the next step above the Sons of the Wolf. He loved the sea and so became a *Balilla marinaretto,* clad in blue and wearing a flat white cap. On Saturday afternoon or Sunday morning, he rode his bicycle across to the Fascist Youth Hall on the east side of Udine to see an inspirational movie, learn the history of fascism, or study the making of weapons and the organization of the armed forces. The study was light, and the boys generally enjoyed the meetings for the chance to march like real soldiers or sailors. In October 1932, when he was twelve, Franco went to Rome for a *Balilla* parade before Mussolini. It was the tenth anniversary of the founding of fascism.

Boys not in the marine branch of *Balilla* trained in the mountains. Probably it was his love of the sea and an antipathy for mountains, rather than any small rebellion against his father's influence, that directed Franco into the marine branch. His part of Italy is a narrow, productive bench between the Adriatic Sea and the rocky *Prealpi Venete.* To enjoy nature, residents go north to the mountains or south to the beach. Franco disliked skiing, and unlike the many Italians who hunted rabbits and hares and even songbirds for sport and food, he had an aversion to killing animals. He did eat meat, though he saw its origins in haunting clarity when he passed a butcher's shop within which the red, peeled hares, hanging upside down by their bulging hind legs, stared like living things.

When he was fifteen, Franco passed the examinations for admission to the Military School of Rome. He began this apprenticeship for his career in October 1935. The routine was tough at Rome and tougher, later, at Modena, where he attended the Royal Academy of Infantry and Cavalry, Italy's West Point; but he did not chafe under it. Other first-year *allievi* got hazed (Franco saw some boys squeezing toothpaste into the rectum of another), but Franco was protected by his physique, by a dignity that could intimidate, and by his position as a star soccer player. His best scholastic subject was drawing. He drew ancient buildings freehand with sharp lines, good perspective, and accurate dimensions. He did not paint, and he says with considerable positiveness that he did not draw for recreation or release.

The fellowship at Rome replaced that of the Fascist Youth, which had dropped him the day he entered the military school—the military organization (except for the Fascist Militia) being separate from the party. And the regimen of the *Scuola Militare* extended that of Ida di Bello. As an instructor of cadets, Franco had to assemble on a Sunday afternoon the seven members of his company who were on punishment and could not have the afternoon off as the others did. One of the seven was missing, with Franco's secret permission. When the officer of the day asked about him, Franco replied, "Sir, he's sick in bed." The officer went to look and found the bed unoccupied. Di Bello confessed and, as he would have done at home, served his five-day confinement in near-cheerfulness. He admired justice even from beneath its heel.

At Modena, pushed through the two-year curriculum two months early because of the army's need for officers, Franco topped his class of 344 in rifle shooting and in athletics, easily winning the pentathlon that amounted to a final examination in athletics. Prince Umberto, a spectator, congratulated him and afterward exchanged several friendly letters with him.

In overall ratings, with emphasis on academic achievement, Franco graduated twenty-second.

Those were good days for him, and better ones followed. Newly commissioned in the infantry, he spent a delightful two-week leave at home. He showed off his uniform to his father, who was very proud, and to his mother; to former teachers and school friends; and to a girl named Miriam whom he met and saw much of during that leave. For him, "bells were ringing, angels flying, violins playing." Miriam was Di Bello's first love. "The war," he said in a letter years later, "was light years far from me in those days, not only because of my general happiness but also because there were no signs at all in my town of a conflict being in progress."

When his leave was over at the end of May 1941, he reported to the motorcycle company to which he had been assigned and was sent to Karlovac, Yugoslavia, for action against the Communist partisans. Di Bello's platoon of thirty-two men was attacked while on reconnaissance and lost twelve men—seven killed, three captured (never to return), and two severely wounded. Those were the worst losses of any platoon's, and the loss conferred a particular obligation upon the unit. Italian authorities had decreed that civilians caught firing on soldiers were to be tried on the spot and shot. A few days after the attack on Di Bello and his men, four partisans who had lain in a ditch and delayed Italian movements with their fire finally ran out of ammunition and were captured, tried, and condemned. The sentence was carried out in the cemetery of the village, with a burial ditch already dug. Di Bello had the duty of commanding a firing squad of his men. Three partisans died instantly. One lay unconscious but alive. With his nine-millimeter Beretta pistol, from a distance of eight inches, Di Bello as commander of the squad shot the man at the place a doctor pointed out on his head. "I can say that that has been the most awful experience that I ever have had in my life," he said forty years afterward.

During the summer of 1942, he was sent to Rome to prepare for North African combat. In January, he took a train to Sicily for a night flight to Tunisia, wondering as he traveled what would become of his beautiful country, "so incongruous in the role of an aggressor."

> Certainly, I would have done my duty at any cost to defend it, but I wasn't going to do so: I was going, as I had been in Yugoslavia, to a Country which had not anything to do with mine, to fight against people whom hadn't shown any aggressive intentions toward my Country, people I didn't hate simply because I hadn't any reason to hate them. This all was mere thinking, of course, because loyalty and duty were both beyond question, but I couldn't stand asking myself, above all, the WHY of my situation at the moment.

In Tunisia, he fought a civilized war compared to that against the partisans—"We knew where the enemy was." On May 7 came news that American troops had taken Tunis. On May 11, having lost contact with headquarters, Di Bello had his seventy men in a wadi waiting for capture. They had burned their documents and destroyed their weapons. They had no ammunition, no food, and no gasoline. When two soldiers in a British armored car appeared, scavenging for captives, Di Bello went out to meet them, not raising his hands or making any other sign of surrender. The noncom who addressed him in high-school French did not point a gun at him. Surrender was the order of the day and needed no formalities. The noncom drove off and returned, hauling four barrels of gasoline. *"Vous allez* Medjez-el-Bab,*"* he said. Di Bello and his men drove, unescorted, to Medjez-el-Bab and confinement.

Di Bello was glad to learn that his permanent stay as a prisoner would be in the United States, whose newness and power had excited him since childhood. But the violence and misery he experienced at two other North African camps under American control did not reinforce that excitement. On July 21, 1943, Di Bello embarked from Oran on a Liberty Ship. The trip was as bad as the African camps had been: pitifully little food, only twenty minutes of fresh air a day, heavy seas, and "awful news about Sicily, awful news about Italy." Mussolini fell on July 26. Di Bello was seasick all the way across the Atlantic. At Norfolk, Virginia, where the ship docked, there was an overnight wait on board with no food or fresh air.

Everything seemed brighter the next day. The prisoners were taken into a pavilion on shore, deloused, and given a shower, the first in months for Di Bello. "Everything was so neat and orderly, big and wealthy, strong and plentiful that I couldn't do without thinking again and again how stupid a nonsense it had been for my little and poor Country to fight . . . such a powerful, civil, and immense Country." A poster showed an American warplane going down in flames, with the message, "Someone talked." Di Bello sounded it out: "So-may-oh-nay tal-ket." A beautiful language, he decided. Before boarding a train for the camp at Como, Mississippi, the prisoners got a good meal, finally, and were "treated as civil and human beings." On the train ride, Di Bello had his first iced tea, which he liked, and he absorbed the views.

At that point, captivity could have looked worse. It got worse, of course. Di Bello dared it to do so when he unhesitatingly crumpled his collaboration form that fall. That action, which in view of his loyalties he could hardly have failed to take, put him in motion toward the camp on the Texas plains that became a holding area specifically for Italians who, like Di Bello, refused to cooperate with their captors.

THREE

Italy's surrender to the Allies on September 8, 1943,
following by a few weeks the deposing of Mussolini by
the king and the Grand Council of the Fascist party,
humiliated Di Bello and thousands of his fellow
prisoners in the United States and elsewhere. They
had grown up in a country where, as Di Bello wrote,
"people had come to really believe that they hadn't
anything to worry about since there was somebody
(Him) who took care of worrying for them and who,
after all, had remarkably improved their situation in
the last fifteen years." Even when involvement in the
war was near, they thought that "He knew what He was
doing, He knew that the war wouldn't have lasted
more than two or three months and then we would
build an Empire at 'the price of a couple of thousand
dead,' so no one was worried more than normal and
people came to fully rely upon the Wehrmacht in a
foolish spirit of 'zusammen mar[s]chi[e]ren' to victory." To Di Bello, the mistakes of Mussolini may by
then have begun assuming the character in which he
later saw them:

He wanted to change a People of artists, artisans, sailors, fishers, singers and dreamers into a People of warriors . . . ! Ridiculous! The Italian of our times is the heir of the Renaissance, not of the Roman Empire, his culture has roots in the medieval Communes, not certainly in the Rome of Julius Caesar. But, as a true Italian himself, the Man refused to look at reality; he was a dreamer himself, a visionary.

The Fascist regime held

an orgy of parades, military ceremonies, huge gatherings of people, bellicose speeches and so on: it was a style which finally turned out to be kind of a "status symbol" of the Regime. In other words, the project was to give a military outlook to the nation, not actually to militarize it. To "look like" was more important than "to be," so the propaganda reels, for instance, always showed a people in a perpetual ready-to-fight attitude: things Italian style . . . !

But if Di Bello and his stripe of prisoner saw fault and error in their country's past leadership, it was as part of a double image, and a subordinate part. The dominant part, whether or not exactly in the form of a familiar thrust-out jaw, reminded them that they were still soldiers bound by oaths of loyalty and that the justification for a sudden change of loyalty was by no means clear. Italy, with the south a born-again ally of yesterday's enemy and with the north under German domination through the figure of the rescued Mussolini, was divided as in a civil war. What had happened to their families on either side of the line, many of the prisoners had as yet no idea, though Di Bello got his first letter from home on October 1, 1943, a little less than five months after his capture.

Depressed but also entrenched by these develop-
ments, Di Bello and his kind found themselves under
pressure from their own generals and colonels to
renew their oaths to the king of Italy, which is to say,
to the pro-Allied government of southern Italy. Those
who did not do so would be considered traitors and
Fascists, and upon their return to Italy would be subject to court-martial. So they were told. In the camp
at Mississippi, where Di Bello was sent from Virginia
and spent most of his first months in the United
States, the persuaders made themselves cardboard
badges with the heraldic crest of the Italian monarchy
drawn on them in colored pencil to wear on their
clothing. Di Bello was among the thirty-three percent
of captive officers[1] who refused to renew their oaths
or to wear the emblems. He saw his stand—at least,
he sees it now—as based primarily on consistency—on
adherence to the rules under which he had entered
the confrontation. The fact that his family in the
north of Italy might suffer if he took a stand for the
southern government could hardly have escaped his
notice, and the same circumstance must have been a
factor in the decisions of others. Still, there were collaborators from the north and resisters from the
south. There was room for debate over the worthiness
of the rule-givers and the rules, but Di Bello had company in his soldierly clinging to those rules.

Then the real pressure began. It came from
Americans bearing promises of great freedom and
other benefits for those who would join Italian Service
Units and work for the Allies.[2] Those who did join

were sent to various posts around the country and overseas for jobs in supply, engineering, ordnance, and transportation. Those who would not sign ended up (or, if they were already there, stayed) at the Hereford camp.

Before the factions were thus officially separated, they had separated themselves. Di Bello remembers little quarreling, but as squadrons of signers marched off for shipment to their Italian Service Units, he heard his fellow *Nons* shouting at them: *"Servo! Lacché! Lustrascarpe!"*—the last in reference to the holdouts' claim that officers in the service units would be made to shine the shoes of American enlisted men. Di Bello's great bitterness is still against the high-ranking Italian officers who pushed for collaboration. He scorns them as opportunists seeking preferential treatment both during captivity and after the anticipated Allied victory.

Even at the time he understood the temptations, and in fact the sound arguments, for lower-ranking captives to sign the forms. Some of them had families in the south and had no way of knowing whether or not they were safe from retaliation. Di Bello, understanding, wished his collaborating friends at Como well and ceased to consider them friends. He and they stayed on their own sides, and, if they met, said only *"Buon giorno."* Not yet as withdrawn as he would become at Hereford, Di Bello did occasional sketches for a handwritten paper put out by prisoners and called *La Vispa Teresa* (Happy Teresa). The paper itself expressed his side's viewpoint on the big issue, though most of Di Bello's sketches for it were non-political. It was posted with a guard in the daytime on the wall of a barracks near Di Bello's and taken down at night for safekeeping.

At first treated with gratifying respect by the Americans after refusing to collaborate, Di Bello and other *Non*s from the Mississippi camp were sent to Monticello, Arkansas, at the end of March 1944, about five and a half months after refusing to sign. Soon an official of the collaborationist Badoglio government of southern Italy went to the camp to evangelize. He was received with hisses, jeers, and whistles-through-the-teeth by soldiers in a compound near Di Bello's, and he gave it up, not going on to other compounds. During Di Bello's stay of a little over a month at Monticello, a good many holdouts did decide to sign: not he.

He and a trainload of other *Non*s, as they called themselves, marched out of their compound to clapping and shouts of *"Bravi! Bravi!"* from a gallery of enlisted men and left for Hereford.

They had a civilized ride of two nights and parts of two days across Oklahoma and the Texas Panhandle, arriving at the stop near Hereford at seven o'clock on the blustery morning of May 3, 1944. As they marched into camp at the end of the flat, three-mile hike from the tracks, they sang the Fascist anthem "Giovinezza." The officers watching them from Compound 4 joined in the song, giving the straight-armed Fascist salute in welcome. Now Di Bello was confirmed in the fellowship of the *Non*s, in the camp that was more and more being set aside for that kind. For a year he lived in reasonable comfort and sufficiency, keeping himself occupied, avoiding agitators, and seeing no sign that anything harsher than heat waves and sudden storms might emerge from the clear, thin atmosphere of that high-altitude camp.

Franco Di Bello in the early days of his captivity.

FOUR

There were in fact rather constant storms going on around Franco Di Bello: storms of protest, threat, and lamentation. Somehow they left him untouched. Di Bello was not a man to whom things happened. Both his physique and his attitude shielded him from insults and familiarity, though he had to put up with the bumptious shouts of "Hey, *paesà!*" from Neapolitan-Americans among the guards. He was only twenty-three when he arrived at Hereford. He had a quiet, firm voice, suited to the career as an army officer that he had sought unwaveringly since childhood. His bearing and movements suggested the skills that had gained him athletic honors at Modena. He was a large man by the criteria of the 1940s, five-feet-ten and about 185 pounds, black-haired and with a glow of warmth and health beneath his skin. His courtesy, itself an insulation, stood out; in a compound that stayed military through a long captivity, he was a particularly consistent user of *"Lei"* instead of *"Tu"* to superior officers. In all his time as a prisoner, no violence or abuse except for one spontaneous shove (in a North African camp) were ever offered him. The lone shove, coming as it did from an enlisted man, rankled him for years.

The commotion that Di Bello managed so well to ignore was once more an outgrowth of the bitter differences between noncollaborators and collaborators. In the early months of the Hereford camp, prisoners of both persuasions were present, though the Americans tried to segregate them and to ship the collaborators to service units. Clashes between the factions produced outcries so loud and numerous as very possibly to impair the credibility of the later protests about the lack of food.

When collaboration forms were being circulated at Hereford, for instance, a prisoner reported to the camp commander (in an anonymous note in Italian) that "intimidation, acts of aggression, and threats of reprisal" had prevented many officers from signing.[1] Another note, signed only, "Democratic Non-commissioned Officers," told the commander that the writers wanted to be given a chance to collaborate. "We are many," the note said, "and we desire to be transferred away from Hereford"[2]—away from the noncollaborators like Di Bello. A lieutenant sent a note saying he had been slugged by a captain of the Fascist militia for refusing to sing "The Legionnaire's Prayer" at the end of mass. (The song had patriotic and political overtones for the prisoners.) "I've been suffering for thirteen months of great moral torments because of my reservations as an officer P.O.W.," the writer said.[3] Another said the *Nons* dominated the compound:

"I beg you to separate us from this group of fanatics, who are provoking us continuously."[4]

Threats filled the air. Action was much rarer. Nobody was killed or seriously beaten by his fellow prisoners. An American captain at Hereford took club-bearing guards into the officers' compound to supervise the removal of twelve prisoners who had signed up as collaborators and whose preparations for departure had drawn a crowd of demonstrating *Nons*. The captain gravely offended the prisoners' highest-ranking officer, Brigadier General Nazzareno Scattaglia, by threatening to throw him in the guardhouse if he didn't get the demonstrators off the street in a hurry. The threat—this was what really seemed to matter—was made in the presence of other Italian officers. His dignity wounded, the general protested to the Legation of Switzerland, which dealt with Italian prisoners' concerns.[5] The captain said in reply to the protest, "We American Officers took an unlimited amount of verbal abuse by all the Officers of that Compound, and the verbal abuse may be supplied if the Legation wishes. I consider my behavior of a much better type than those of the Italian Officer Prisoners of War that we have at this camp."[6]

Di Bello, having ignored such uproars in their own time, has the impression now that they never happened, that the *Nons* did not make things tough for collaborators. Obviously they sometimes did. The Italian general and the American captain, for example, agreed that a demonstration against the collaborating officers had taken place. Di Bello, always respectful of age and rank, liked and admired the general, by the way, and it may be significant that he did not consider him a Fascist, even though he had observed the general's practice of leading the salute to *Il Duce* at the end of assembly. The ritual ended with a unison *"A noi!"*—"To us!"—the Fascist motto—accompanied by the straight-armed salute.

By Di Bello's definition, a Fascist in the prison-camp days had to be an agitator like a certain Captain Roberti, whom Di Bello thought disdainful and did not like. He liked better the camp's leading Communist, a Lieutenant Ravaglioli, though despising his politics. What were Communists doing in this supposedly Fascist camp? Why wouldn't they sign up to help the Allies, including the Soviet Union? Because they hated capitalism, Di Bello said. In that camp, there were fences of ideology inside those of barbed wire. Then there were privacy fences like Di Bello's, which kept growing taller.

It was strange that Di Bello and his countrymen should turn up as prisoners in such a setting as the Hereford camp. Italians scarcely existed among the civilian residents of the Texas Panhandle, who except for the settlers of three or four enclaves such as Umbarger were predominantly Scotch-Irish in influence, with the ways and speech that their forebears had brought with them from Arkansas and Tennessee. Those residents who had any image of Italians at all thought of them, most likely, as uneducated, cheerful, sweaty, garlicky, and funny. But Di Bello's compound mates, being officers, had to have had at least two years of college. They tended more toward an articulate gloom than ebullience, and at least in the case of the many north Italians, looked nearly as Anglo-Saxon as most Amarilloans and would have found Texas chili and tamales intolerably spicy. The prisoners, though not on the whole religious, came from a wholly Catholic tradition; the Panhandle was as heavily and devoutly Protestant as Ulster. (As such, it seemed almost alien to the largely Catholic Umbargerites.) Whereas in Italy any village might have a thousand-year-old bell tower and be surrounded by vineyards cultivated for centuries, children of the Panhandle's first European settlers were still in midlife, and much farm land was being plowed for the first time as farmers drilled wells to bountiful irrigation water. In Italy, the prisoners had seen the sky always shaped and domesticated by hills and by tile-roofed edifices. Here it was the sky that controlled the empty countryside, for days in succession unimpeded by even a cloud. When the sequence did break, it was with sudden attacks of wind, rain, hail, dust, or snow—an amazing violence to have come out of such sterile air. The captors had had a reason for putting these representatives of an old civilization in the middle of this new, powerful land: escape would be hard and unrewarding (though not impossible, as several of the prisoners proved.)[7] In the absence of that reason, irony would have served as well.

FIVE

Although Americans were generally hostile toward the presumed Fascists who predominated for the last year of the camp, there were pleasant encounters between captor and captive in the earlier days. A tough little guard from upstate New York, Don Houle, admitted years later that he "would as soon knock one of the prisoners in the head as look at him," and he said he proved his willingness during one of the riots. Another time, though, he took a group of "king's men"—collaborationists, as opposed to "Mussolini men" such as Di Bello—to work on a farm. A prisoner who spoke good English told him to go and sit in the shade next to the barn; when it was time to quit, the prisoner would come and get him. And that was the way it worked out. Dozens of such stories grew out of the use of prisoner labor on the farms. The prisoners were generally a lighthearted lot in those days, singing in the fields. At the end of the day when they climbed into the truck to go back, one of their number would wave a make-believe rifle at the others, hurrying them along—maybe saying, "Come on, come on!" This was the phrase used by impatient guards to hurry prisoners, and the syllables became the term for a guard: *"Caman."* [1]

Farmers noticed that prisoners at work among the feed shocks on a farm always dropped everything when they saw a wild animal, especially a jackrabbit. This was before the time of *la fame,* but for sport or because of hunger remembered from childhood, they formed a predatory ring and closed it, walking toward the center till the rabbit, running this way and that without finding a passage, finally made a dash and was caught, screaming, and clubbed.

The superintendent of streets and grounds at the camp, a civilian named Guy Lawrence, sometimes took prisoners to his house briefly during a working day. This delighted them because they could pick up and hold the superintendent's daughter, who was two or three years old. Obviously, these were "king's men." But there was a "Mussolini man" among the prisoners who were put to work building a swimming pool for American personnel. (The Army called it an irrigation pool; a swimming pool was not authorized. There was a tennis court at camp, too, but it appeared on inventories as "caliche storage.") This man, troublesome as all his kind appeared to the superintendent, pushed his wheelbarrow of cement up the ramp with intentional slowness, blocking traffic. The superintendent borrowed a loaded wheelbarrow from a worker and started up the ramp behind the blackshirt. He whistled once, got no response, and then rammed his wheelbarrow into the prisoner's back as hard as he could charge. The prisoner toppled six feet to the ground, wheelbarrow and all, and thereafter, the superintendent found, behaved much better.

The hospital at camp had its own fence and gate and was separate from the four prison compounds. Prisoners considered it a desirable refuge. One who did his best to stay there as long as possible was Lieutenant Giuseppe Berto, who later became one of Italy's most respected novelists, partly on the basis of books he wrote at Hereford. He went in for an operation on a double hernia he had incurred in a soccer game. Recuperating, he fell in love with Esther Klinke, a blonde nurse whom the prisoners called "the white angel" for her hair and her sympathetic ways. Berto suddenly decided that a wound to his right foot had developed complications. That required another operation. Afterward, it occurred to him that his appendix needed removing. The surgeon disagreed.[2]

Back in his compound, Berto wrote "The Seed Among the Thorns *(Il seme tra le spine),*" a short story based on his stay in the hospital and his unreturned love for the nurse, who is "Miss Lane" in the story. Miss Klinke attributed her patient's protestations mainly to loneliness, just as Miss Lane in the story does. Until the plot of the story was summarized for her nearly forty years afterward, including a description of her allergic sniffle and the vertical furrows in her brow, she had had no idea that a prisoner had really been in love with her, much less written a story about her. "I guess I missed my chance," she said.

Like Miss Klinke, the other nurses made allowances for the prisoners' loneliness. This was just as well. If a certain pretty blonde, for instance, had taken every prisoner's confession seriously, she would have had to consider herself the cause of several ruined lives and perhaps a death or two. She got many letters from stricken prisoners:[3]

> When I can, alone, I wacht your picture talking with you, very easily, in italian for hours, telling all what I think, what I wish, what I hope.

> You have plaied with my heart, so a naughty child . . . . I love you more of my life!—I am very grieved and flee you for not to suffer. I will not you forget.

> I destroy your letters with the death in my heart. . . . The stove complains they are few.

Prisoners who worked in the American part of the camp sometimes got to talk with women (though this was against regulations) and now and then even found the chance to be alone with one. Mostly they looked and wished. The sergeant of the mess hall for civilians, Grant Hanna, observed his prisoner KPs after they had helped serve at a party. As soon as the guests left, the prisoners rushed over to sit and squirm in chairs where the women had sat. One prisoner, so the story goes, got the chance they all dreamed about and then rejected it. At a party, he sneaked into a closet with a full-chested female employee who had a crush on him. After a moment the door banged open and she came practically flying out. The prisoner had discovered that the fullness was factory-made.

Within their compounds, the Italian officers had decent and fairly private quarters.[4] Each "box," one-fifth of a barracks partitioned off, accommodated four officers in its one main room and two bedrooms; each bedroom had two wooden cots. In the main room were a coal stove of the kind found in railroad depots and country stores, a wooden table, sometimes an ironing board that swung down from the wall on hinges, and one or two wooden stools or chairs. Each bedroom also had a table and a chair or two, the number depending partly on what the officers chose to make for themselves; sometimes they illegally tore up the boardwalks for material.

Franco Di Bello's quarters were at one of the vortices of creative activity. On a table in Barracks 555, Berto composed his novels and short stories, writing with a pen in a loose-leafed Royal Composition book bound with a black string. One of the novels became widely known as *Il cielo e rosso,* but the title referred to the sky at home in Italy, red with the fire of bombing raids as Berto had read and heard about them, and not to the sky above him then, which the wind in spring made red with dust. Until the last, hard months of camp, when his creative impulse became dormant, Berto wrote much about wartime Italy, setting *Il cielo* in a city recognizable as Treviso, which is near his home town, Mogliano Veneto.

Berto took his manuscript, a few pages at a time, to Barracks 558, cocking his unkempt blond head as he listened to the temperate criticism of Di Bello's roommate, First Lieutenant Aurelio Manzoni. Manzoni knew something about literature and practically every creative and scholarly field. He was a short man with ruddy cheeks lifted in a half-smile that could express at the same time an attentive regard and a keen skepticism, qualities well suited to the serialized discussions that took place in the barracks. Sometimes Di Bello read Berto's latest pages, but he might not join the talk. He was not much on literary and political conversation.

During Di Bello's first year in the Hereford camp, and in fact for the first two years of the camp's operation (from the spring of 1943 to May 1945), the prisoners had plenty of first-quality food.[5] Di Bello and the other officers of Compound 4 brought volunteers over from the Italian enlisted men's compounds to do their cooking. For extras, the officers could buy sweets and, for a time, even beer at the post exchange, using the coupons given them in lieu of the pay to which they were entitled under the Geneva Convention.

Di Bello spent a good part of his leisure time playing soccer and volleyball; he was one of the two best soccer players in the officers' compound, by his own estimate and by one of the minutely detailed game stories that prisoner-reporters composed for the handwritten camp newspapers. Another large part of his leisure was devoted to reading Saroyan, Steinbeck, and Hemingway, looking up the foreign words in a foreign *Webster's Collegiate Dictionary*. But he gave still more attention to a new diversion, oil painting. He got paints, canvases, and brushes through the PX, and he found an empty barracks room to use as a studio.

Considering his captive state and the terrible news about Mussolini's assassination and the defeat of the Axis powers in Europe, he thought it not a bad time, that year ending in May 1945.

S I X

Until the last month of spring in the last year of the war, the Hereford prisoners, touchy and voluble as they were, had complained about the food at the camp only among themselves and only in a casual way, as any soldier does. They had plenty of food, in fact. The Geneva Convention required that America give its prisoners food of the same nutritional value as American soldiers were given.[1] This seems to have been done during most of the existence of the Hereford Camp. The officers of Di Bello's compound and the enlisted men of the other three compounds had managed to Mediterraneanize the truckloads of Texas beef, Kansas flour, and California squash and carrots that regularly came to their commissary. Di Bello, who liked to eat and whose waistline readily bulged when he was not playing enough soccer, volunteered to help make *tagliatelle* of flour and eggs on Saturday nights in his mess hall for Sunday dinner. The perquisite was the chance to enjoy a mess for himself at midnight when the work was done. American employees of the camp loved to be invited to eat in the prisoners' mess halls, and they reminisce about the great platters of spaghetti that both they and their hosts ate.

It was so until the war ended in Europe and Allied prisoners were liberated. American prisoners set free from Orb, from Ziegenhain, told of having eaten pine needles and twigs.[2] Americans at home saw pitiful pictures of them in *Life* magazine and in newsreels. And what were Axis prisoners in the United States eating? The same food that American civilians were eating, and even food the civilians saw little of: butter, chocolate, steak. The public wrote angry letters to editors. Indignant columns by Drew Pearson and Walter Winchell were rebutted in a *Commonweal* editorial deploring vengefulness;[3] but orders went out for prison-camp commanders to reduce rations.

Some of the Hereford prisoners, until then, had passed the time by taking care of a variety of animals, not all of which can have returned much affection. There were black-widow spiders, for instance, and at least one rattlesnake. Di Bello, who cannot bear to think of animals suffering, once watched the owner of the snake put a live gray mouse into its box and shut the glass lid; the snake slithered forward, and the mouse, cornered, turned pale as it awaited the strike. "A terrible shock," Di Bello says of the experience.

A pet more in the prisoners' tradition was Camilla, the sparrow that an officer, former commander of a submarine, caught young and tamed. Standing outside among hundreds of other officers, Camilla's owner would turn her loose and watch her fly. At a whistle from him, she would pick him out of the crowd and land on his shoulder.

The one civilian in the compound, an effeminate fellow, suspected of homosexuality by other prisoners, who before his capture had been a correspondent for the Italian wire service Agenzia Stefania, had a pet cat. The bird inevitably disappeared, and the submarine commander held a trial in the absence of the correspondent. The cat was found guilty and promptly hanged. The correspondent, though about forty years old, not in good health, and temperamentally no warrior, confronted the executioner in a rage. The two agreed to fight a duel with sabers after repatriation. Like so many fights that soldiers swear to have after they are discharged, this one seems never to have come off. If it did, the word never got around to Di Bello or his friends.

Another pet raiser, a pianist for whom some others had chipped in and bought a piano so he could practice, kept four or five dogs in his room. They disappeared—whether during or before *la fame,* the time of hunger, nobody seems to remember. Perhaps they were victims of nothing more sinister than an order forbidding prisoners to keep pets anymore. But there is no doubt about what happened to most of the other four-footed pets that prisoners kept into the late spring of 1945. They ended up as clean bones underneath the barracks.

If the order relayed on May 4 from the Eighth Service Command in Dallas had been meticulously carried out, the cats and dogs would have survived. The order instructed commanders of prisoner of war camps to limit the rations of prisoners who did not work to between 2,300 and 2,500 calories a day. Working prisoners were to get 3,500.[4] Those are enough calories for young men of average weight. But because the camp commander stubbornly refused to observe the condition of his prisoners, whom he disliked and (with some justification) considered crybabies, rations at Hereford were kept short of these allowances, especially for the officers. Even the unauthorized food the prisoners sought out did not make up the deficit.

On May 8, 1945, an enlisted sailor from Calabria got a paring knife and, standing outside a barracks in Compound 2, stabbed a corporal in the heart. Former prisoners say he was angry because the corporal had not given him enough of some caramels he had. The corporal, a slender young man from Barlassina with long arching eyebrows and a thin mustache,[5] died a few minutes later on a bunk in the barracks. The murderer was sentenced to life imprisonment in the federal penitentiary at Leavenworth, Kansas. There, according to Di Bello, who investigated the inmate's death, he eventually killed himself by jumping from a high window.

At the evening count two days after the stabbing, the compound leader, Sergeant-Major Giacomello Carlo— his name deserves recording because of his evident good will and good sense—spoke to the men. He deplored the emotional atmosphere that had "cut off the existence of two of our fellows, that of the victim as well as that of the guilty one."[6] The prisoners must not be self-elected judges and force their ideas upon others, he said. They should put a stop to all the "discourse of killing this one or killing that one, these continuous allegations about someone selling himself to the enemy, that someone is a traitor"; must accept the fact that the war was over and that "we've been conquered;" and must see their own faults as a people and eliminate them "if we expect history to record a new victory for us." Temperance of this kind prevailed in deed if not in words; only the one death of violent causes occurred in the camp. To judge by Carlo's remarks, it must have arisen from political differences as well as from hunger.

With the tightening of rations, prisoners turned their attention to the effects of hunger on themselves. Men lay enervated on their bunks for hours in the daytime. When they had to walk to the latrine or to the sorry meals in the mess halls, Di Bello remembers, they did so slowly, conserving energy, looking at the ground like men who have received bad news from home. Di Bello's roommate was a young professor and lawyer of such mental vigor that he claimed to be able to free his body of fever by mere will power; but he could not control his subconscious, and at night he dreamed of great North Italian feasts. Two rows of barracks from Di Bello's quarters, Giuseppe Berto, the writer, had a strange response to hunger: his veins popped out in prominent blue ridges, so that when he stood naked he looked like a manikin in an exhibit on the workings of the circulatory system.

From Fort Bliss, Texas, the commissary at Hereford had acquired a tremendous supply of salted herrings. Each fish was about eleven inches long, as the former post quartermaster, Benjamin T. (Tol) Ware of Amarillo, recalls. Officers sat eight to a table in their mess halls, and sometimes the entree for an entire table was one herring. ("They had to have their pickled herring," a Hereford man who used to work at the camp said. Most of the American personnel at the camp seem to have known nothing of the conditions inside the prisoners' compounds.) There was other food, but far too little. For the enlisted men and noncoms, rations were more generous, according to some former occupants of their compounds; Di Bello says prisoners in Compound 3 threw food over the fence to the officers in Compound 4. Some enlisted men complained of hunger, though, and food throughout the enclosures was certainly far scarcer than before. Scrounging, theft, and improvisation became aids to survival.

Not much of the outside food consisted of dogs and cats. A roast small animal makes an entree for only a very few men. The same is true of rattlesnakes, which several officers ate. Grasshoppers provided good protein, but very little of it. Di Bello scorned the grasshopper-eaters as show-offs, dramatizing their hunger. Eating a grasshopper, he said, is "like eating a bean." Certain officers fried them in brilliantine, available at the PX. The identity of one of the grasshopper-eaters provided ironic pleasure. Lieutenant Paolo Foscari, a descendant of a Venetian doge, starved into eating bugs! In spite of Di Bello's scorn, he considered the reduction of food a serious matter, and with his big appetite and muscular body he was affected by *la fame* at least as much as others.

The herring days provided a bonus of calories and protein for those willing to accept it. Some of the officers, including a lieutenant from Di Bello's home city of Udine, dug fish heads and entrails out of the kitchen waste and boiled them for broth. The same Udinese found a chance to pick up extra food when he helped to plan and build, in a field just east of camp, a concrete memorial to the five prisoners who had died during their captivity at Hereford. A soldier formerly under the lieutenant's command in North Africa was working in an American mess hall. When the work party of ten, under guard, walked past the mess hall on the way to the memorial, the lieutenant would beat on the side of the bucket in which the tools were carried. At the signal, the mess-hall worker would come out with bread and potatoes. The guard, fortunately, didn't care.

That was one of the best vehicles to a better diet—an unconcerned guard. Another was a job in town or on a farm, where there was often extra food from the civilian employers. But this was only for enlisted men. Officers, under the Convention, cannot be made to work for their captors, and these officers, full of non-collaborationist zeal, certainly were not going to volunteer to help the Allies. Prisoners who worked in potato sheds around Hereford, the center of a rich produce-farming area, were blessed. The seventy-six-man shifts of prisoners employed in a shed at Dawn, a town between the camp and Umbarger, were allowed by the operator of the business to build a campfire and boil all the potatoes they wanted in a ten-gallon bucket. Sometimes the proprietor would buy bread and meat for them, too. The case of one private showed that there were hazards as well as opportunities in connection with outside work. The farmers sometimes gave food to him and the other field workers, but once, when a farmer insulted them, the private, along with other prisoners, went on strike for the rest of the day. He was subsequently sent to the guardhouse for fifteen days of bread and water.

Maybe that incident illustrates a self-created hazard. The prisoners were not required to take the insult so hard. In that sense, they often made things worse for themselves. "It should be remembered that Italians in general are very sensitive and find it hard to endure captivity," a Red Cross inspector of the camp said.[7] For some of them, words must have eased the strain. During the period of *la fame*, prisoners complained not only to each other but to the Red Cross, the U.S. Provost Marshal General's office, the Italian Embassy, and friends and relatives outside the camp. Or so they thought. It turned out very often that they were complaining to the wind, and an angry wind, too, in the form of American authorities who flung the letters into their faces. Some of the letters are in the U.S. Army Military History Institute at Carlisle Barracks, Pennsylvania.

A sergeant wrote to (he thought) his mother in Naples that he was confined "in a tropical region in the State of Texas, where the heat is 45 C degrees [113 F] in the shade" and that the daily diet for each man consisted of a handful of cereal and half a salt herring. If the report of the diet is as imaginative as that of the climate, then the facts would add some calories. The climate and terrain at Hereford are more like those of Denver than those of the tropics.[8] In any case, the letter was condemned by authorities in Dallas and sent back to the commander.

So was a letter from a lieutenant to his brother in Avellino, saying it would soon be noon and "you cannot imagine how I will swallow the eleven spoonfuls of floating macaroni, the four small slices of potatoes and the spoonful of pot cheese or the one-fourth of a pilchard."[9]

Another lieutenant tried to write his aunt in Boonton, New Jersey. He asked a fellow prisoner to mail the letter for him outside the compound, but the friend was caught, relieved of the letter, and put in the guardhouse. The lieutenant had written that since the end of the war in Europe, the prisoners had undergone "great reductions in our food allowance and the absolute ban on the sale of foodstuffs in our canteens" and had not been allowed to receive packages from friends and relatives. The reasons for the restrictions, he said, were unknown. "We only know that they have been applied with intentional dastardliness . . . to inflict sufferings upon human beings without defense and without protection, guilty only of having done their duty as combatants in war, and of conduct always conforming with their sentiments as Italians and therefore of non collaborating voluntarily with the captor."[10]

Berto, the novelist in the barracks near Di Bello's, quit writing fiction after May, when *la fame* began. He was too listless from hunger to bestir himself, just as the young pianist with the gift piano had to break off his daily practice. Berto did write a letter, though. It was addressed to an acquaintance in Buenos Aires who seems to have been connected with an international relief organization, and it said, in the version of an American military translator:

> Dear Tito,
> once again I am compelled to ask you for something. I am ashamed to do so, not only because I am afraid that I will never be able to repay you, but above all, because I fear that somebody else might be in need more than I. Still, if it is possible without too much sacrifice on your part, try to send me some food-stuffs through your Committee or the Red Cross. If the requests from Africa have diminished, send more to us. I hope you will understand and excuse me.[11]

This was not one of Berto's more eloquent works, but then, it never reached its intended audience. The censors condemned it.

SEVEN

For all his drawing courses in school, Di Bello had
never studied painting. At Hereford he ordered
brushes, colors, canvases, an easel, and turpentine
from Sears, Roebuck and Company through the PX
and in the fall of 1944 began practicing and studying.
He worked in the empty room of a box that had only one
occupant instead of four, and he a friend of Di Bello's.
The draftsmanship came easy; Di Bello had always had
a steady, accurate hand. At first he drew, rather than
painted, using a brush and a single color at a time.
When one color was dry, he added others singly.

Varying the colors, getting them true, was not so
easy, but he had help from a talented officer who lent
him art books and made suggestions about blending.
Before long, Di Bello the pupil was doing portraits
from faces and from photographs. His new interest
helped him pass the long days at camp, and in the
hungry period, his quiet absorption contrasted with
the behavior of a good many of the other prisoners,
who seemed to find a catharsis in outcries. Di Bello
refused to wallow in captivity. He did not pin pictures

of Betty Grable or Lana Turner to the wall in his barracks room, and he ignored the morning and evening parade of pretty clerks and nurses going to and from their jobs in the American part of the camp. (Other prisoners, however, lined the compounds to yell and whistle.) He did not even put up photographs of his parents and brother back in Udine. In letters home, he avoided mention of conditions during the last months of camp, even when things got so bad that he rather expected to die.

Things could hardly have been as bad, after all, as some of the prisoners made out. Nobody starved to death at the Hereford camp. Nobody went home looking all shins and elbows and eyes, as American soldiers looked when they were set free from German camps. Italians have never been famous for understatement, and Di Bello, who today has lost much of his regard for his countrymen and would like to live in the United States, seems to feel particularly alien to Italian exaggeration and emotionalism. Even in his prisoner days, when he burned with loyalty to Italy, he turned back the theatrical laments of some of his fellows. "It wasn't all that tragic," he says of the deprivation, and he must have given the same response to his friends' laments at the time.

He did reveal his feelings, however, in a self-portrait he made at the height of *la fame.* Compared to photographs made before and after the hungry period, the face did not look particularly thin, and the cheekbones had no more relief than normal. But the dark eyes were sunken and constricted, as if by fever, and the face had creases in it that in such a young skin suggested much worry.

Di Bello's art teacher at camp was Achille Cattanei, a gentlemanly little major who with his wife had operated an interior-decorating studio in Milan before the war. Cattanei was in his late forties. Though he did not do many originals, he had a well-developed gift for reproducing paintings by the masters. He made many such reproductions in camp. And he put together five coffee-table-size books, bound in canvas, that preserved some of the best creative work of the compound, including a Berto story, *"È passata la guerra,"* that was in one respect a joke. In discussions, Di Bello's roommate, Manzoni, had expressed a distaste for Steinbeck, whom Berto liked; and so, after writing *"È passata,"* Berto presented it to Manzoni as his translation of a new Steinbeck story. Manzoni read it and pronounced, "At last, Steinbeck has learned to write." The story went into Cattanei's anthology, and Berto's writing set out firmly in an American direction. Manzoni, now a successful lawyer in Milan, owns a volume of the Cattanei collection. It is art in itself, as a medieval manuscript is.

With sports almost out of the question after *la fame* began, Di Bello lost himself more deeply in art than he had ever before done in any nonessential endeavor less active than soccer. Hunger and the bad war news contributed to a quiet revulsion from which art seemed a more and more acceptable refuge. Di Bello painted the quizzical face of Manzoni and the Irish one of the tall and blond Lieutenant George H.

Dinan, a former prison warden from Massachusetts whom most of the Italians liked and considered kind. Seeing such portraits, other American officers asked him to do theirs. The signature "d i b 1945" turned up in more and more lower left corners. The officers paid him not in the forbidden money but in goods, especially candy and other food. (They were not really supposed to do that, either.[1]) One gave him a box of oil colors. Another gave him a novel.

Among the officers for whom Di Bello did paintings was the chaplain, an Ohio priest named Achilles P. Ferreri, who was distressed by the prisoners' hunger—this was in the late summer of 1945. When Ferreri asked what he could do in return for the paintings, Di Bello had a quick answer.

"Father," he said, "I'm hungry. Give me something to eat."

The chaplain did so, and on more than a one-time basis. He asked Di Bello and his best friend to come to his office for two hours every morning and translate a New Testament into Italian—a pressing task, he assured them. Neither of the Italians had any systematic religious beliefs, but it didn't matter. They knew the assignment had been made only so the chaplain could give each of them two doughnuts and a glass of milk every morning. This went on for a month.

Ferreri knew that there were many talented painters among the officers. It seemed a good time to have their work shown; it would help keep their minds off food. Would Di Bello help him set up an art show? With his linguistic and artistic ability, his leadership and efficiency, Di Bello was well qualified to do this, and he agreed. The show was held in August in an empty barracks at the north end of Compound 4. There were 220 works on display, mostly paintings but also pieces of sculpture, wood engravings, and a few objects of handicraft. Di Bello had one work—an oil portrait of a "man in burnoose."[2]

The show was open to the public, and one extremely interested visitor was the Reverend John H. Krukkert, pastor of St. Mary's Church in Umbarger. He had been invited by his friend Ferreri. Formerly a church builder of considerable attainment in the big Diocese of Amarillo—a noted bargainer in such projects, too—but lately limited by poor health to the unchallenging assignment in the isolated little parish, Krukkert can't have looked at the exhibition very long before beginning to envision a work that would glorify God, constitute an enduring bargain for the parish, and for a while keep his mind off his boredom and his aching joints.

The priest and the chaplain got the necessary authorization, which in view of the unprecedented nature of the project must have contained some more-than-ordinarily evasive language, even for the Army.[3] And the chaplain asked Di Bello a question: did he know some prisoners who would be willing to use their talents as painters and carvers inside a Catholic church in a little town near camp?

Di Bello said he would ask around. He went first to Cattanei, the courteous painter who had helped him. Fine, said Cattanei, but they also needed a painter who knew how to do murals. That would be

Dino Gambetti, a bushy-browed engineer officer from Mantua, who as a professional painter in civilian life had already done frescoes in churches in Genoa and Turin. He taught the composition of oil paintings to prisoners (one of the many college-level courses given in camp by various officers[4]), and he painted pleasing small oils on flour sacks, signing them with his prisoner- identification number, 28359. Di Bello did not know Gambetti and felt diffident about approaching him—a captain. So Cattanei took over that piece of recruiting. He also got word to two noncommissioned officers who came from wood-carving villages in the North.

So the executants were lined up. But painters would need help with cleaning brushes, mixing paints, and moving scaffolds. So they told themselves. Knowing that the women of this little town were to serve a meal to the workers every day, the artists chose as one helper a fellow who would particularly appreciate the blessing. He was Leonida Gorlato, a tall, big-framed captain. Gorlato was Cattanei's roommate, and Gambetti also knew him. When Gambetti was painting in his studio in an unused room in a barracks, Gorlato would regularly drop in, though he was no painter himself. He wanted to see if Gambetti was doing a still life that day, as he often did, on arrangements of fruit brought to him by an American officer. If so, Gambetti would give him some of the fruit when he finished painting. Although Gambetti was an undemonstrative and even dour man in those days (he became open and cheerful later, as Di Bello found to his surprise when he went to Genoa in 1982 to talk with him), he had strong sympathies. Perceiving that this big man suffered more than the ordinary degree of hunger, Gambetti asked that Gorlato be named one of the helpers.

Di Bello chose the other. It was easy. His best friend, a generous, laughing first lieutenant from Naples, could clean brushes as well as anyone else. The friend, six years older than Di Bello, was Mario de Cristofaro, dark and narrow-faced, a classic south Italian. Though his manners confirmed his upbringing as a member of a noble family, de Cristofaro laughed and joked in the way expected of any Neapolitan. "You could tell from a mile away that he was from Naples," Di Bello said. They called each other "Fra" and "Mariu" in the Neapolitan way. Before *la fame,* the two played soccer together and, especially, volleyball, at which de Cristofaro was a good and rather hard competitor in spite of a general laziness.

De Cristofaro considered himself an energetic Neapolitan, an oxymoron that he explained thus: the lazy Neapolitan gets up in the morning, opens his window, and says in a slow, contented way, "What a brilliant sky! What a beautiful day! I can't work on a day like this—I'm going back to bed." The energetic one looks out, sees the sun, and fires off, "Whatabrilliant skywhatabeautifuldayIcan'tworkonadaylikethisI'mgoing backtobed." Like his friend, de Cristofaro had right-wing political beliefs. He was proud of his several years' military service, thought Italy and Mussolini had made a big mistake in entering World War II, and, again like Di Bello, stayed out of prisoner-polemics.

So five Italian officers and two noncoms were ready to start work on this most unusual of all Father John Krukkert's church projects. There was an obstacle, though. How could *these* officers, for all this time noncollaborators of a holy zeal, now suddenly consent to work for their captors? When Di Bello and the other two artists were called before the camp commander, they said they would decorate St. Mary's "only," as Di Bello recalls, "on condition that our effort should be considered as a personal performance for the sake of Christian brotherhood and of mutual comprehension, not as a form of POWs' cooperation." And they stipulated that they would accept no pay. The commander agreed to these conditions with what Di Bello took to be an open appreciation of the prisoners' position. It seems a strangely generous attitude for Colonel Joseph Ralph Carvolth, but no matter.

One more member of the party had to be chosen: the driver who would take the artists to and from St. Mary's and guard them on the job. Ferreri, the chaplain, had a candidate—an amiable sergeant from Pennsylvania, assigned to a headquarters detachment at camp and not a guard or a driver by either Army training or civilian experience. He was a faithful Catholic, though, and had been a pleasant occasional helper around Ferreri's office. Of course, the assignment would be no great blessing to the sergeant, who had plenty to eat and who could leave camp any time he was off duty and go home to the room that he and his wife rented in Hereford. But when the chaplain approached him, the chance to do a service to his church appealed to John Coyle. He was an agreeable fellow, in any case. He said he would do the job.

John Coyle knew the prisoners were hungry. When he supervised the loading of food carts that prisoners daily pushed to the commissary, the prisoners shook their heads and told him, "Not enough." He knew some Italian. In spite of his sketchy education, Coyle liked words—he uses them with fluency and precision today—and the flowing sounds of the prisoners' language charmed him. Unlike most of the American noncoms and enlisted men who often came into contact with the prisoners, Coyle respected them, tried to be friendly with them, and soon learned enough Italian to converse a little with them. If a zealot snubbed him, he shrugged and went on. He noticed the disappearance of cats and dogs from the compound and knew what it meant. He could do nothing, but it distressed him to think that men were hungry. Even the casual insults—"Wop," "Dago"—that many guards directed toward the prisoners upset him. Coyle considered all people to be alike, and he assumed that these Italians had no more wanted to be in the war or in this camp than he had. The second part, at least, was wrong: they *had* chosen, in their way, to be at Hereford. But most of the American soldiers at the camp were like Coyle in knowing little or nothing of the background of the prisoners.

While he was working in Ferreri's office, Coyle enjoyed talking with two Italian enlisted men who assisted the chaplain and who were learning English (he did not meet Di Bello during this time). He got them food from the chaplain's cabinet. Ferreri didn't mind; he and Father James Salvi, a Franciscan friar who often came to the camp, deplored the underfeeding of the prisoners. Salvi often smuggled food to them in his black mass kit. But American officers and soldiers might have objected to the snacks in the chaplain's office, or at least might have felt it their duty to report the prisoners, and to report Coyle, too. Once, when Ferreri was out of the office, one of his assistants had a piece of pastry in one hand and a jar of peaches in the other. Coyle heard a faint footstep outside. *"Ascolta!"* he hissed. The prisoner grinned at the joke and kept on eating. There was a knock at the door. Tumultuous haste; food clattering back into the cabinet. The knocker came in: only Ferreri. *"Mamma mia!"* the prisoner said. Then he started cleaning the spilled food out of the cabinet. No one knew why Ferreri had decided to knock—maybe out of mischievousness.

Ferreri and Salvi had shied away from making official protests about the prisoners' rations, but they wrote to the bishop of the Amarillo Diocese confirming the inadequacy. They said getting a detailed report on calories and on the men's condition was hard because they were not authorities on such matters and "because the American authorities insist that the Prisoner are receiving all the consideration that they are entitled according to the present regulations." They added: "We know that some of the American officers are as convinced as we are that unwarranted hardship is being imposed upon the prisoners, but that they are unwilling to make official statements of their convictions."[5] Some of the prisoners thought Ferreri's reception of their complaints was ambiguous, and a priest accused the chaplain of partiality to the collaborators.[6]

But after all, the *Nons* were sometimes bitterly hostile to Americans, and the collaborators, by definition, were friendly. It would have required a good bit of saintliness to stay altogether impartial. Certainly Di Bello and de Cristofaro, though dedicated noncollaborators, got kind treatment from the chaplain.

A week before the project at St. Mary's was to start, the three artists made a reconnaissance. Under the date October 15 in his "One Year Diary," Di Bello wrote in Italian: "With Cattanei and Gambetti I am taken in the chaplain's car, in absolute liberty, to the Umbarger church that we have been asked to decorate." The three took measurements, assessed the needs for materials and colors, and listened to the parish priest's suggestions in regard to subjects and placement. Then the artists "had another experience which we hadn't had in the last two and a half years: we sat at the table of Father Krukkert and were *served* a magnificent lunch. It was a great day, the first in years which gave me the feeling of having come back to my normal status of a free and dignified individual." Back in camp, the artists had a week to make preliminary sketches and plans. Gambetti did most of this.

The war with Japan had been over for two months. In the comics, Joe Palooka and Jerry Leemy were mustered out of the service. ("What a gorgeous day," Joe said.)[7] An Amarillo colonel returned from a long imprisonment by the Japanese during which, he said, for a period of seven months his battalion held at least one funeral every afternoon (and once nine funerals) for men dead of starvation and overwork.[8] A photographic studio advertised in the Amarillo Daily News: "Returnees: Be Photographed Before Discarding Your Uniform!"[9] In Germany, the American military government reduced the authorized daily ration for civilians to 1,345 calories, though the rations for displaced persons, as General Dwight D. Eisenhower announced, were being raised to 2,300 a day, and those for "racial, religious, and political persecutees" to 2,500.[10] The Italian word for "rumor" is *voce*. Throughout the Hereford camp, voices of repatriation were mingled with complaints about hunger.

Father Krukkert had spent much of September in California, vacationing and trying to sell a house he owned in San Clemente. Back in Umbarger with the decoration of St. Mary's coming up, he started work. This was his element, a big, tangible project. He took donations, brought back artists' supplies from Amarillo, and put the altar society women to work in the kitchen. Just before the artists were due to start work, he prepared a small basement room for masses. He had a willing farmer make scaffolds so the artists could paint keys and chalices and Pentecostal flames on the walls and angels on the arch of the church. Now Krukkert had the project at St. Mary's ready to begin.

St. Mary's Church in 1991.
(Ron Marlow photo)

Canvas of the Assumption of Mary, centerpiece of the
art works left in St. Mary's Church at Umbarger by
Italian prisoners of war. (Ron Marlow photo)

The main works of art executed by P.O.W. painters at St. Mary's Church. The canvas of the Assumption of Mary is in the center, the mural of the Annunciation at left and that of the Visitation at right. (Ron Marlow photo)

Carving of the Last Supper. (Ron Marlow photo)

Mural of the Annunciation. The crack at right has developed recently from settling of the church. (Ron Marlow photo)

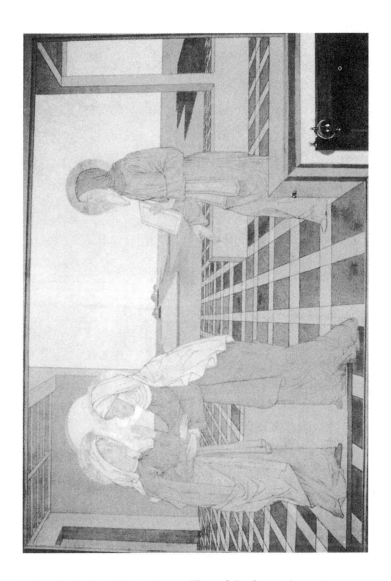

Mural of the Visitation. (Ron Marlow photo)

A sketch of the interior of an officer's quarters in the
Hereford POW camp, drawn by Alfredo Rizzon, a
prisoner.

Another drawing by Rizzon of the interior of a POW
officer's quarters at the Hereford camp.

A third view by Rizzon of a POW officer's quarters at the Hereford camp.

EIGHT

The real Umbarger, though its center was a little plains settlement on U.S. Highway 60 marked by a grain elevator, the church, and a few houses, also included farms for seven or eight miles around. The community had grown by accretion and not with an inspired rush as in the case of some of the south Texas German towns. Settlers from Germany and Switzerland came on propitious or necessitous occasions over a period of decades, the word of the good cheap land attracting them and that of the Roman Catholic and German-speaking background of the residents persuading them. They established their farms and tethered them to St. Mary's church. The Protestant families with names such as Donnell, Hancock, and Dowlen that resided inside the geographical perimeters of the community belonged in only that way—geographically. The eighty families that attended St. Mary's were Umbarger.

St. Mary's had had John Krukkert as its priest only since the beginning of 1944.[1] He must have started planning improvements, or wishing he could plan them, as soon as he began holding mass in the drab sanctuary. Krukkert liked color. He had designed and built his own house in California—a white stucco, with three tiers of landscaped yard, deep in brilliant flowers, and with a tiled patio that looked over the edge of a cliff to the green Pacific. He lived there seven years in near-retirement because of a mysterious ailment, painful and debilitating. Then, because of the wartime shortage of priests, the bishop of Amarillo called him back to the diocese. Krukkert was reluctant to go. In West Texas he would have no ocean, few flowers, and no house of his own. But he went, filling a chaplaincy and serving as an assistant pastor for a time. He could no longer get out in the field as he had done in the 1920s and early 1930s when the Amarillo diocese was new, building churches and rectories with zeal and ingenuity, often against resistance based on anti-Catholicism.[2]

On January 17, 1944, Krukkert became pastor at Umbarger. His predecessor, John Dolje, another Hollander, had died six days earlier at the age of eighty-three—the oldest priest in the diocese—and was buried next to the church he had built.[3] Dolje had come to Umbarger in 1916, when settlers were still trickling in from the Midwest, from Schulenburg and other Texas German towns, and from overseas. He started his pastorate in a white wooden church south of the Santa Fe tracks and moved north to the new brick building fourteen years later. For long periods during the rest of his life he refused his own salary in order to help pay off the debt on the church while his parishioners raised money with picnics, dances, and door-to-door solicitations. The debt was retired in 1943.[4] Now there was nothing for Krukkert, the builder, to build. The drabness inside St. Mary's is bound to have disturbed him, but bargains in churchly ornament did not grow in scrap piles. He did not have a lot of money, since *Casa de las Flores,* as he had named the San Clemente place, had not been sold. It was over a year before the art exhibit at the Hereford camp showed him the way to his next labor.

The days in this quiet pastorate flowed placidly into each other. Crying babies were the most common disturbance, and as a remedy Krukkert had only to stop preaching and pointedly wait while the mother took the disturbance outside. It's doubtful that he ever had to wait long. Krukkert could be charming, but until he smiled he seemed on the point of finding out the guilt of whomever he looked at. He had close-together eyes, rimless glasses, thick eyebrows that stopped abruptly in the middle of their outward arches, a wide, thin mouth, and a wart on the left side of his nose.[5] He was the priest who asked the Amarillo visitors why they didn't go to their own church. But that was not just Krukkert; that was part of being in Umbarger, where the populace consisted of those who had sought out like minds and were on guard against the influence of unlike ones. The familial wall of German Catholicism sheltered the community from the winds of Protestant error and Scotch-Irish untidiness, and even from encroachment by faithful outsiders.

The wall did have two sides. During World War I, Umbarger accents aroused hostility when farmers took their eggs and cream to market in Canyon or Amarillo. One farmer had to hide beneath a haystack to save himself, it is said, after making a remark about a Canyon soldier whose death had occurred not in combat but in an accident. Well, then, the farmer is supposed to have said, "he vasn't a hero, vas he?" By the time of World War II, feeling against Umbarger people as Germans had subsided. After all, the community sent plenty of its own to the service, as the stars in parlor windows showed. And Umbarger people were largely peaceable, honest, and hard-working.

In bad times at Umbarger, jackrabbits throve. (Jackrabbits are really hares, much like the ones in the markets of Udine.) They stole wheat, oats, alfalfa, and grass. Farmers and ranchers held drives, walking in a single rank miles long and flushing thousands of rabbits to be killed with shotguns. Some people ate jackrabbits, usually after soaking them in vinegar or milk to remove the wild taste. More often, farmers cut them up and fed them to hogs and chickens. Wildlife biologists consider the jackrabbit a "weed animal": it increases, like certain weeds, with overgrazing, since it likes sparse cover through which it can see a coyote approaching, or a man. Umbarger people, with a few exceptions, have always been farmers more than ranchers, and fluctuations in jackrabbit population in their land must have more complicated causes. In 1945, Krukkert's second year at St. Mary's, there were jackrabbits everywhere.

NINE

As a driver and guard, Sergeant John Coyle was not exactly typical. He had scarcely driven a truck before, and on the first morning of the project at St. Mary's he had to study the diagram on the dashboard every time he shifted gears. He guarded his detail by asking the men every morning how they were, whether they had heard from their families, whether they needed anything—and by concealing his weapon from them. Di Bello, the only English-speaking prisoner among the group of artists and their helpers, rode with Coyle in the cab, and he never saw a sign of a weapon. He soon realized that it represented, to Coyle, an unwanted power over his fellow men. Coyle confirmed that impression four decades afterward: these were members of a sensitive race, he said, and it would do special harm to them to "go lording around with that thing."

He knew, anyway, that it would be a bluff if he did make a show of his gun. "Suppose one of them broke and ran," he said. "I wasn't going to shoot a man for that." But he couldn't remember what kind of gun he had been issued; couldn't remember a gun at all. That many years back, a memory can't search and discover, and Coyle, in interviews or in letters written in his amiable and modest scrawl, has not been as lucky with chance recollections as Di Bello. Di Bello's focus has been kept sharp by his diary and by the significance of that episode in his life, confinement naturally making more impression on a prisoner than on, say, an administrative employee of the jail.

After checking out at the main gate of the prison camp, Coyle drove the truck along narrow paved roads six miles to the little ranch and farm town of Hereford. He was slender, wavy-haired, and blue-eyed, and he had a bass voice that was musical but flattish in inflection, an earthy, droll sound. He said "dese" and "dose"; he had only an eighth-grade education, having dropped out to go to work in a knitting mill and help support his mother and younger brother. On that frosty[1] morning of October 22, he talked with his easygoing, self-deprecating warmth to Di Bello, but there was as yet some distance between them, the result of their difference in rank and of their having just met. "Lieutenant" and "Sergeant," the two called each other. Otherwise, neither of them remembers any longer what they talked about the first day.

From Hereford, they went twenty miles east on U.S. Highway 60 to Umbarger. The chief landmark in the town was the church, a tan brick building with a belfry rising well above the tops of the Siberian elms at its sides. That did not mean that the belfry was tall, only that the elms were not. Just the same, the two men in the cab of the truck could see the church for several miles as they approached it. The plains there descend from the west so gradually that they seem flat, but the view eastward is the longer one. No trees obstruct it, except for the planted elms and hackberries around the farmhouses.

The truck pulled up and stopped on the church grounds. Very probably it was met by Krukkert, who is bound to have been excited by the prospect that his church was at last about to be made beautiful, and at very little cost. The women of Umbarger were curious about the new element that was to be part of the life of the community for the weeks to come—these foreigners whom they were to feed like exotic harvest hands and from whom, as a matter of prudence, their daughters were supposed to keep their distance. The Umbarger men were mostly at work in the fields or at their jobs in the grain elevator, the store, or the garage. Some were still overseas, since Umbarger, almost exclusively of German and German-Swiss origin, had contributed at least its share of men to the fight against their cousins' land and its allies. The children, those too young to have dropped out, graduated, or gone to war, were in the Umbarger school two hundred yards east of the church, being taught by nuns. So on that first day, the visitors did not see a large sample of the population.

The prisoners jumped down from the truck onto unfenced earth and inhaled the brisk civilian air. For some, it was the first time in two and a half years to be outside the double fences at the Hereford camp.

Father Krukkert had brought a pickup load of artists'
and carvers' supplies from Amarillo, thirty miles away.
There were cans of tempera paint and tubes of oils,
heavy *carta da spolvero* (like brown butcher paper),
brushes and turpentine, and cans of powdered charcoal. Then or a little later, there was a supply of light-
colored wood (probably basswood, the American
linden) bought by an old-time Umbargerite from a
firm in Amarillo that made counters for stores. This
was to be used for a carved relief of Da Vinci's *Last Supper.* From nearer home, the same Umbargerite also
provided oak for other carvings; it came from some
one-by-six planks that he had bought to make a cow
pen. The prisoners spent the morning unloading
these supplies and laying them out in the drab little
church, whose milky windows sapped the light of the
plains sunshine. They did not hurry; Umbarger
people remember that during the early part of the
project the prisoners distressed the priest by dawdling.
And after all, why should they unduly exert themselves?

Dinner, as the big midday meal is called by Texas
farm and ranch people, was to be in the basement,
where Krukkert had had a long wooden table set up.
Under his direction, the women of the altar society at
the church had made duty schedules for preparing
meals. They were not rigid schedules. The priest's
housekeeper, Mathilda, was to be a constant presence,
and various women were to come and help when they
could make it. The women would provide roasts,
hams, sausage, salads, homemade bread, sauerkraut,
mashed potatoes, homemade jellies and jams, and

pies and cobblers from home-grown and home-
canned cherries. For setting, serving, and clearing,
there would be help from several teenage girls.

At noon, the seven prisoners went down the stairs
to the basement. They very likely had not smelled the
food, since it was prepared in the rectory, a few steps
behind the church. The women and girls had carried
it in platters and bowls through the back door and
down the back stairs to the basement. The prisoners,
after Krukkert had blessed the food, ate it so ravenous-
ly that he worried about their harming themselves and
admonished them to slow down. There were chickens
for the entree, and the trimmings included sweet
potatoes baked in their skins, a dish that Di Bello, for
one, had tasted only a few times. Coyle ate with the
prisoners and was not surprised by their painful enjoy-
ment of the meal. He knew something of the conditions at the camp. Umbarger people who dropped in
wondered at the appetites and the loose belts. The
trousers of Major Cattanei, who had been small to
begin with, billowed out from a waist as spare as a
cornerpost. Yet only a few Umbarger people seem to
have suspected, on the basis of what they saw, that
there was any serious lack of food at the camp. They
knew that American captors fed prisoners better than
the prisoners were fed in their mothers' kitchens.

Those Umbargerites who saw the artists at the
beginning of the project took with them an impression of hollow-eyed men who stared. The prisoners
seemed distant. Even John Coyle found most of them
so. Gorlato, the big one, was downright surly. Gam-

betti, the pro, kept to his work and wasted no smiles. Cattanei, though gentle and courteous, had an aristocratic reserve unlike the easy ways of Pennsylvania factory workers or Texas farmers. Even Di Bello, with his good English, and de Cristofaro, whose warmth needed no language, were relatively reserved on that first Monday. The noncomissioned officers, Carlo Sanvito and Enrico Zorzi,[2] kept to themselves and their separate work and for a time had preparations to make in another part of the settlement. Among themselves, the prisoners observed rank as if in camp. Gorlato made it clear that he was to be called *"Lei"* by the two officers he outranked—Di Bello and de Cristofaro. He helped only Cattanei, the major. De Cristofaro, a first lieutenant, therefore helped both Di Bello and Gambetti.

A day or two showed Di Bello what kind of guard he and the others had in John Coyle, "an intelligent, sensible, civil, marvelous man whom we all admired and loved." Coyle's interest in their comfort and well-being particularly impressed the group. "Nobody had treated us like that for years," Di Bello said. In the truck on the second morning, after the first greetings of the day, Di Bello said, "Come on, John, don't call me anymore lieutenant, call me Frank." The artists soon understood that Coyle was not one of the jumpy *camans*. He told Di Bello, who told the others, that he trusted them; and they knew that if they escaped, or sneaked off with one of the local girls and got caught, Coyle would have to pay. "We would not have done that to John Coyle," Di Bello said.

The two carvers, needing special knives, went across Highway 60 to Henry Bracht's Umbarger Welding & Machine Shop and made them out of files and saws. Nobody objected to their having such an array of edged and pointed tools; Father Krukkert had said these were good men. Coyle made no effort to go and watch over them.[3] Bracht said he even took the prisoners into his house and showed them his collection of hunting guns. He was one of the most recent immigrants from the old country, and he felt a kinship with the prisoners. He managed to talk with them—"You alvays find vords what you can translate," he said. Bracht's wife, Amalia, spent many days in the rectory helping cook for the prisoners, once making them pies of cherries she had harvested from her three trees. In the church, she watched the carvers for hours. One of them in particular, though unable to converse with her, would look up every now and then and give her a big smile.

Soon the prisoners began to loosen up and to get acquainted with Umbarger people. The Umbargerites, too, had had some reserve to overcome, as Di Bello said:

> It was really new for those people to see and meet this new species of human, the prisoner of war, whom everyone had heard about but nobody had ever seen. It seems natural to me that in the mind of the good parishioners of St. Mary's we should have been sort of a mixture of mysterious, legendary and a little bit dangerous too (after all we had been the enemies of their Country) so, no wonder that some of them was even somehow reluctant to approach us. On our part we

were extremely curious to know how the first impact with this new people would be, what relations would we be able to establish and develop with this people or former enemies. But this problem was soon to reveal itself an inconsistent one, since for some reason (evidently much stronger than diffidence, prejudice and hatred) a spontaneous stream of good feelings began almost at once to flow among us. Not a single word about the war and the past, we were here for a work of peace and love, not a word of reproach, we had already suffered for years from lack of freedom and from separation from our families, not a word of blaming, because now we were there to work for them and their community.

At first, the Umbarger people asked mostly about the prisoners' families and what the war had done to them. After a bit, they began asking "lots of questions about Rome, the Pope, Florence, Venice, the funny form of our peninsula, etc." But ultimately,

their great interest was that we were artists and that we were going to paint all that enourmus blank surface of their church, so they stood for hours watching us while we were on the scaffolds painting and they asked a lot of questions about the subjects we were painting, how we mixed the colors, how we chose the brushes and so on. Of course this reciprocal interest was soon to become a general friendly relation and in many cases a true and durable frienship.

In the preparation of meals,

every family was in competition with the others on whom served "the artists" the best and the most sophisticated . . . ! Marvelous people! Think that in those first days we were positively hungry after months of quasi-starving and this wonderful food which was offered us was health and for us, a real blessing which probably saved the life of some of us.

An exaggeration, this last, since none of the artists' countrymen back in camp died of hunger. But certainly the food was a blessing, as was the spirit in which it was given.

Names were hard for both parties. Italian had nothing like Brockman, Bracht, Hoffman, Skarke, or Hollenstein, and for Umbarger people the names of the prisoners all flowed together into a liquid sameness. Jerry (for Geraldine) Skarke, a shy girl of eighteen who came to help on the days when her mother did so, happened to hear an artist casually call across the church to another, *"Eh, bambino!"* She helped serve lunch after that. The prisoners were in an ecstasy over the food and the presence of the girl in the neat skirt and blouse, with a ribbon in her hair, who moved close to them with her pitcher. In the bull's-eye of the full silence that she was helping to create, she came to the man she had heard addressed and asked pertly, "More tea, Bambino?" An explosion of laughter burst from the table, and she fled.

Surprisingly, the only prisoner who could have caught her by the hand and explained, subduing his own laughter, did not do so. Di Bello would have taken a special pleasure in this; he was the youngest of the seven and so the nearest to her age, and in her freshness and vulnerability she impressed him as a most beautiful girl. She ran across the space of the lawn between the back of the church and the rectory kitchen, where the food was prepared, and nothing her mother said could persuade her to go back to the table that day.

On other days, when she was to serve and walked across the back of the sanctuary, Di Bello called out to her—"Where are you going tonight?" "Going to the dance?" "Is your boyfriend coming to fetch you?" (He did not know that her boyfriend was still overseas with the Seabees.) And she would call something back, shyly but in the spirit. The other artists made prisoner-remarks among themselves about the girl; for Di Bello, the fact that he was a sort of ambassador, was in a church, and had met her mother kept his admiration more on the respectful side. (For a few days while hunger still had priority over other drives, all the crew was practically without libido, and this was the case a good while longer for those in camp.) Just the same, he noticed her *belle gambe* right away, hemlines being fairly high at the time. His correspondence with Miriam, the girl he had met during his wonderful leave after military school, had sputtered out, and she was separated from him, anyway, by several thousand miles. This girl was an element of the new and restorative landscape in which he found himself. Di Bello told himself that he was "a little bit in love" with Jerry Skarke. But in the whole forty-one working days, they were alone together only once, and only for a moment.

TEN

Aside from John Coyle and the chaplain, another good Catholic much interested in the welfare of the Hereford prisoners was Laurence J. FitzSimon, bishop of Amarillo. Brought up in Texas, FitzSimon had spent five years in training at Rome when he was a young man, and the Italian he learned at that time served him when he visited the Hereford camp, as he did a good many times. On one of his early visits he picked up a guitar he saw in one of the compounds and sang and played *"O mia bela madunina,"* a song in the Milanese dialect. On September 26 of that first year he confirmed 122 prisoners.[1] His involvement with the camp extended also to its American personnel. In June 1943 he tried unsuccessfully to save the job of the commander at the time, Colonel Ralph Hall, who in fighting bitterly to get a United Service Organizations (USO) center opened in Hereford had roused such hostility among local Baptists that the Army thought best to transfer him.[2]

FitzSimon, half Irish and half German by descent, was born in San Antonio and grew up west of there in

Castroville. He was ordained in 1921, had pastorates in south Texas towns, and in 1941 when he was chancellor of the Archdiocese of San Antonio, heard on his car radio that he had been made the third bishop of Amarillo. In that capacity, he lived in a brick mansion on diocesan property in Amarillo. He worked mornings in the chancery on the same property and spent the rest of the day and often much of the night at home working on his collection of documents on the history of the Southwest.

At work, FitzSimon was businesslike and sometimes impatient. His sternness and stateliness could frighten those around him. Callers had to have appointments. Of average size, FitzSimon had an oval face and a strong chin, wore gold-rimmed glasses, and combed his short hair straight across the crown of his head. He spoke precisely and did not joke. He did have diversions: he played a small organ in his house, composed a *"Tantum ergo"* and an *"O salutaris,"* and made useful objects of wood and metal in a shop in his basement. He was politically conservative and anti-Communist.

On September 5, 1945, the bishop wrote a long letter to Congressman Francis E. (Gene) Worley, whose district took in the Panhandle. FitzSimon had discovered *la fame* at the Hereford camp. One of his informants was the Reverend Joseph Saraceno of Brooklyn, who in June had preached at the camp (and its branches at Dumas and at Amarillo Army Air Field) and who said men collapsed from weakness as he preached.[3] The bishop also had seen a report by a prisoner, Major Luigi Cabitto, head physician of the officers' compound, that the average daily caloric value of food assigned to the compound from the first of June through the first two weeks of August had been from 2,096 to 2,142, with some days' rations as low as 1,500; prisoners had lost an average of twenty-two pounds each, he said.[4] By the time the bishop wrote the congressman, the prisoners had been hungry for more than four months.

At the time he wrote the letter, the big art show was over, and Krukkert, along with Chaplain Ferreri, had taken preliminary steps toward putting some of the talent to work. It would be a month before Di Bello, Gambetti, and Cattanei made the first reconnaissance trip to St. Mary's and had the memorable lunch at Krukkert's.

In his letter,[5] FitzSimon took care to praise the commander, Colonel Joseph Ralph Carvolth, and to make clear that he did not blame Carvolth for the conditions he had found. He told the congressman that in the past he had found the prisoners happy and well-treated. Even after hearing that the camp had been reserved for Fascists and was by then "filled with the criminal Fascist element," he got the impression on a visit in the spring of 1945 that the prisoners were as contented as could be expected. "I could learn nothing about the reasons why these men were placed in a separate class," he told Worley, "or how they had been approached by our Officers when they had to declare their political beliefs. At any rate they had then no reason to complain about their treatment."

A few weeks later, the bishop began hearing reports of scarce food, of closed canteens, of an embargo on packages from outside, and of severe treatment by the guards. "This new policy came after our V-E Day and shortly before the discovery of the horrible atrocities the Nazis had practiced on their prisoners," he said. To investigate, he visited the camp on July 5, 1945, accompanied by Chaplain Ferreri.

I immediately noticed a changed attitude. I spoke to groups in the barracks chapels, but my words had no apparent effect. Many just stared at me in a sullen, defiant attitude; others turned their faces away; some cried. There wasn't much that I could say either when I heard from individuals what had happened. I finally visited the Italian Officers' compound, where I spent some time to learn the whole story. The first complaint was the food . . . . Since about V-E Day the rations have been reduced to the minimum necessary to sustain life; nor could the prisoners satisfy their hunger by purchasing in the canteens or receive any parcels of food from outside. Such parcels were, I was told, returned to the senders. At noon I had lunch with the prisoners. We were served a bowl of weak watery soup, containing pieces of gummy-like spaghetti, but absolutely tasteless, as the concoction was made without any salt, or so little that it was most unpalatable. After this dish-water soup, we had each a dry over-salted herring. I saw some of the men hold back their soup for the herring course and dip a herring into the soup to give it a little salt. Then we had bread and water and that was all. After saying our prayers, we left the mess hall. I was then interested to know what would be served for dinner. I was shown the contents of the kitchen cold-storage room; in it I saw some tubs of pigs feet, sacks of moldy looking potatoes and a basket of over-ripe tomatoes. After talking with the prisoners a while, I visited the hospital. I am glad to say that I heard no unusual complaints from the patients about their treatment there.

Since that visit, the bishop said, he had heard reports of prisoners' being beaten with clubs and being confined in an unroofed enclosure for forty-eight hours during a rainy spell, with no protection but a small burlap tent swung from the fence.

> I wish to say, dear Mr. Worley, that both as a Christian and as an American I am greatly distressed by the manner in which we are now treating these prisoners. Someone may ask me if I have not heard about the barbarous manner in which the Nazis and the Japs have treated the prisoners. Certainly I have heard of it and I have seen the pictures. I would believe these reports even without testimony, since the authors of these crimes are Nazis and Japs. These modern barbarians have inflicted tortures on their own people. We must conclude that they are either rising from savagery, as are the Japanese, or have fallen back into savagery as have the Nazis. They are cruel and inhumane. So were the Indians of our Plains. But we are Americans. We have professed a high and noble attitude to the vanquished. We have distinguished between the guilty and the innocent. We take pride in the fact that we can be as great in victory as we were in the prosecution of the war.

FitzSimon said the Hereford prisoners had been guilty of no war crimes and had "fought because they could not do otherwise." Furthermore, he said, he knew of no reports that American prisoners of war in Italy had been harshly treated. Mistreating the

Hereford prisoners was not only inhumane but stupid, he said.

> Before the new regulations went into effect, I believe, from my own personal observation, that almost everyone of the prisoners could have been converted to our side. We could have made them our friends and sent them back to Italy to become the strongest supporters of democracy and American ideals. Now they are beginning to hate us; they asked me why all this is done, and to my utter confusion and shame I could not give them any answer.

He said he could not help suspecting that the new policy had "been dictated by certain anti-Christian elements in our country whose outpourings of hatred toward our broken enemies do not express the great heart of America." It was too bad, he said, that the originators of the policy "and possibly with them the 'Brass Hat' in Washington who issued the order" could not be compelled to visit the Hereford compounds and see the effect of the policy. He said "our men at Hereford" were in no way responsible for "the treatment they must give the prisoners."

> Colonel Carvolth is, I believe, a real gentleman, but he and his men are "under orders" from Washington and I presume occasionally some Inspector comes around to see that these orders are obeyed.

The bishop said he unfortunately could not enclose any supporting statements from Ferreri or from the Reverend James Salvi, the Franciscan who often held services at the camp.

I must say that both of them are afraid to be quoted and will not sign any statement. It is a sad state of affairs when two real men of God are in such fear of Army Regulations that they must refuse publicly to support a cause that should appeal to every man possessing the feelings of humanity. I often wonder what might have happened in Germany if a Military Chaplain had complained about conditions at Buchenwald . . . . I wonder what would have happened to a Catholic Bishop over there who would have written such a letter as this. He would have ended his days (and I was told some Bishops did, with many priests) in the same camp whose atrocities he had condemned. I do not wish to infer that Hereford is another Buchenwald, but it is a dark spot of this war and a disgrace to our country.

He said he regretted that the diocese and a Panhandle town had become associated, even in a small way, "with the history of the war's unforgettable crimes." He asked the congressman to get something done to remove "this stain" on the nations' war record, and he added:

Do not permit . . . these men to return to Italy without removing from their minds a most bitter memory of Texas and our Panhandle. The good people of Hereford are probably unaware of what is going on in the gloomy stockade south of town; it is best that they do not realize that the name of Hereford is held in execration by the miserable broken men who spend their cheerless hungry months behind the tall barbed-wire.

This was a devastating letter, and it did not matter that FitzSimon could only guess at the origin and spirit of the order to reduce rations. He did not recognize the impact that public pressure had had on the

Army. Of course, shortages of food for American civilians had done nothing to reduce the pressure. In New York, Mayor Fiorello La Guardia ordered meatless Tuesdays and Fridays for restaurants. (After proprietors protested that the shortage of poultry, along with black-market trading in fish, had made it hard for them to comply, he relented and allowed the serving of liver, oxtails, tripe, and sweetbreads on those days.)[6] The United States faced the most critical shortages of food, and especially meat, in its history; so an Army spokesman said in April 1945 as he announced that the Army thenceforth would limit meat in prisoners' diets to hearts, livers, and kidneys and would use substitutes for scarce foods.[7]

Some reductions in rations had been ordered before the uproar about coddling began. Almost a year earlier, in fact, the Provost Marshal General's office authorized commanders to "alter the menus of prisoners of war in the interests of food conservation" and ordered that the cost of rations for prisoners never exceed that of rations for American troops. In the spring of 1945, the allowance of meat was set at four ounces a prisoner a day. "This policy," an Army spokesman said, "has been adopted as a food conservation measure." Perhaps so, but the spokesman, Brigadier General B. M. Bryan, assistant provost marshal general, in explaining such policies to the House Committee on Military Affairs, showed a keen sensitivity to public complaints of coddling.[8]

Prisoners, including those at Hereford, generally thought the big reduction after V-E Day reflected both vengefulness and an awareness that the Germans could no longer retaliate against Allied prisoners. "Many of us," Di Bello wrote, "thought it was not worthy of the Americans acting like that." The prisoners at Hereford, and emphatically the officers, underwent shortages beyond those contemplated in the orders from Washington and Dallas. This was by no means true at all camps; it seems to have been so at Camp Trinidad, Colorado, where the German prisoners said they had enough food until V-E Day, and thereafter typically received only porridge and a little milk for breakfast and pea soup, lettuce and one slice of bread for each of the other two meals.[9] But among Italian prisoners of war, the ones at Hereford had the hardship stories that would later shock and surprise those of other camps in the United States. After all, Hereford was what an inspecting officer had called it: "Last stop on road"—the end of the line for noncollaborators.[10] Or for prisoners who were, as the camp commander characterized them, "noncooperative and fascist."[11]

When the order came in from the Eighth Service Command, both the camp commander—Colonel Carvolth—and his quartermaster officer seized upon it as a punitive measure. Both felt that they had reason to do so: their prisoners were "a pretty tough bunch; they were going to take charge pretty fast" if allowed to do so. That characterization was made by the quartermaster lieutenant, Benjamin T. (Tol) Ware, in an interview; Ware is now a banker in Amarillo. (From among this "tough bunch" came the artists and carvers whom

John Coyle daily left unwatched at St. Mary's.) Ware took the order as authority to limit the calories of non-collaborators. "If they would work with us, OK."—If not, here came the smelly herring, barrel after barrel of them. Prisoners, after a while on this diet, would say, "We're going to swim back to Italy." Austerity and monotony were intended, but Ware said neither he nor Colonel Carvolth knew that men were actually losing weight under the regimen. If they had known, he said, they would have modified the order. Ware said the commander questioned him and two American doctors to make sure that the diet was adequate. As to the prisoners' complaints—in Ware's opinion, that was all some of the prisoners had to do, sit and complain.

Carvolth was a National Guard officer, in civilian life a prothonotary in the courthouse at Bradford, Pennsylvania. Some of his fellow officers found him fair-minded, efficient, and rather stiffly agreeable. Others agreed with a medical officer and fellow Pennsylvanian, Captain Charles C. Alfano, who, according to his widow, Louise Alfano, thought Carvolth stupid and selfish, a commander who served himself first at meals and always took the best cut of meat. Carvolth was a short, ruddy man, in his mid-fifties when he took command at Hereford in July 1944, fourteen months after the camp opened. He wore a sandy toupee, which to the amusement of subordinates sometimes slipped. He was one of the last officers in the Army to carry a riding quirt.

Esther Klinke, the nurse, thought Carvolth "a great guy" in spite of his habit of mischievously popping her on the back of her knee with the quirt. Lieutenant Ware, who came from Amarillo, liked him, allowing for the fact that he was "a cold Yankee," and he admired his efficiency. A representative of the Swiss legation who had known Carvolth in more than one command thought him to be "a very able and astute individual."[12] Carvolth had a sort of right to the quirt; he had served a hitch on the Mexican border during World War I. Before taking command at Hereford, he had commanded the largest prison camp in Texas, the one for Germans at Mexia.

Ware considered Carvolth tough with the prisoners but held toughness to be necessary in view of the prisoners' character. Once, a trainload of noncollaborators came in, and on shakedown, though they had been searched previously, were relieved of "knives, clubs, and everything in the world." The first night, Ware said, the newcomers grabbed an American enlisted man and badly beat him. As punishment, they were put into an open field for about forty-eight hours, until they "decided they wanted to cooperate." This was the summer of 1945, after Mussolini's death, an event that Ware said they refused to believe: they would "sing that song about him" and say the news was propaganda. Once when the group was demonstrating and threatening to get out of control, guards sprayed machinegun shots on the ground in front of them. Ware said he did not disapprove of Carvolth's disciplinary measures, and he admired the way the colonel kept close track of equipment, seeing that surplus items were sent back into Army stocks. The camp had been buying its bread on contract, but Carvolth found a way to cut down on that expense.

"You're going to operate a bakery," he told Ware.

"Colonel," Ware said, "I don't know a damn thing about operating a bakery." But he learned, and the operation did save money. Ware found Carvolth aloof, all business, formal at meals, "the kind of guy that probably half of them didn't care for." Perhaps it was his banker's system of values that put Ware in the other half.

Esther Klinke, though she liked the commander, recognized his toughness, his rigidity about military procedure. One of the hospital employees, a prisoner, had been giving penicillin shots on twelve-hour shifts because of an outbreak of infections at camp. When he missed one of the two daily head-counts during such a shift, he was put into the guardhouse on bread and water. Miss Klinke went to Carvolth and complained. He said the order had come from the Eighth Service Command and he didn't know what he could do. She went back to him, pleading, and back once again. Finally he phoned Dallas and got the order softened: the prisoner could return to duty but must take his meals and showers in his own compound thereafter, and not in the hospital compound. But it had required three visits, and by a nurse whom Carvolth presumably liked.

Because Carvolth didn't like onions, Miss Klinke helped him raise shallots and chives. Carvolth did like food; he had brought his own mess sergeant to camp from his previous command at Mexia, and meals were good in the officers' mess, where Miss Klinke, in her ambivalent status of civilian with an officer's privileges also ate. Someone—often Ferreri—offered grace at the meals, before which Carvolth would say, "Be quiet, now, and listen to the chaplain." He liked music, and he took part in dances at camp, sometimes dancing with Esther Klinke. He lived in a small two-room house, practically a shack, across from the officers' club. His wife remained in Pennsylvania while he was at Hereford. His son, Joseph R. Carvolth Jr., nine or ten years old, came out for a visit once, and a prisoner painted the boy's portrait in oil.[13]

According to both civilian and military tenets of command leadership, and notwithstanding Bishop FitzSimon's defense, responsibility for conditions at the Hereford camp fell on one person alone. If the commander did not know how little food the prisoners were getting, and of what wretched quality, he should have known. It was not a concern too trivial for his attention. And he could not have helped knowing at least that conditions needed investigating—he saw the prisoners' letters, even if the intended recipients did not. Probably it was some characteristically rigid adherence to form that kept him from acting; he told prisoners that they were not counting calories according to the system he used, which showed the rations to be adequate. This answer, if it was right, hardly excuses him. He could hear, could

read, and could easily have gone into a prisoners'
mess and eaten, as FitzSimon did.

And for all their theatricality, the prisoners did not
essentially exaggerate their hunger. When
FitzSimon's letter finally produced an inspection of
the camp, the scales in the infirmary of Compound 4
showed that the officers had lost, on the average, twenty pounds each during the twenty-three weeks since V-
E Day. They had average weights of 151.5 pounds at
the time of their capture and 131.6 pounds after the
weeks of short rations.[14] According to the general formula, a reduction of 500 in one's daily intake of
calories results in a loss of a pound a week. Then the
officers' rations, from all sources, had fallen short of
their needs by 435 calories a day apiece. In fact, the
food provided at camp fell short by 435 plus the value
of whatever cats, dogs, grasshoppers, fish-gut broths,
and cadged potatoes and bread a prisoner had been
able to turn up as a supplement. Nobody died of
hunger, true, and medical inspections showed no dis-
eases caused by malnutrition. Perhaps, as Di Bello
says, *la fame* was not a tragedy. But at the time, he
thought it would be tragic: fatal, to be precise.

ELEVEN

The weighing came at the end of the first full week of the project at St. Mary's. By then, the artists and their helpers had had six Umbarger dinners and a great many afternoon sandwiches, cakes, and pies. Two of them, besides, were still benefitting from the month's supplement of doughnuts and milk in Chaplain Ferreri's office. So the scales showed the group to have lost less than the average for the officers' compound, except for Di Bello, whose weight since the capture had fallen from 185 to 165 pounds—exactly the average loss. De Cristofaro's had dropped from 165 to 155, and Gambetti's from 150 to 145. (Major Cattanei, who weighed only 130 pounds to start, somehow missed the weighing. And the records for Gorlato's company—one of four in the compound—seem not to have been kept.) The artists ate less as the weeks at St. Mary's went on, and they lost the hollow-eyed look of the first few days. Di Bello uncharacteristically told Mary Brockman that Umbarger had saved their lives.

The work went quickly, as it had to. Gambetti spread brown paper on the floor and stood on it barefoot. Holding a stick with a piece of charcoal on the end, he drew the sketches of the *Annunciation* and the *Visitation*. Each of them was eight feet high and close to twelve feet across, and both had been inspired by color reproductions in Father Krukkert's New Testament. In the same way Gambetti drew an angel with Veronica's veil bearing the image of Christ's face; an angel holding the I N R I inscription that had hung above the cross; the heads of two airy young angels for the spandrels of the semi-arch high above the nave; and many emblems of keys, chalices, doves, and flames, of grape clusters and vines, and of the palm and crown of martyrdom, all for use in medallions and ornamental panels on the walls of the nave and on the outer facing of the choir loft. All these sketches were of his own conception—guided by Krukkert and his illustrated *Vangelo*—in accord with the calculations that he and the other two had made on their preliminary trip to the church.

While Gambetti did this job, fundamental to all the main works in the project except the carving and the one canvas painting, de Cristofaro and Gorlato on their scaffolds took care of the house painter's job on the ceiling and walls. Di Bello and Cattanei started on the many square feet of painted ornamentation on the walls, some of it in a chair rail going all the way around the nave and some of it in vertical panels. One pattern was the wheat and grapes symbolic of the Eucharist; one was endlessly repeated crosses; and one was stylized lilies set within diamond-shaped borders. These were all done in tempera.

For the repeated cross pattern, each cross was echoed in a thin outline like a double image; but the lines that made these cross-shaped husks continued without a break, zigzagging through the display. A close look at the diamond-shaped group of four crosses in isolation reveals a swastika in the middle. The form is American Indian and not Nazi, since the arm at upper left is horizontal. Di Bello knew this, but he took a mischievous pleasure in the pattern anyway. He was still an Axis soldier.

When the sketches were ready, Di Bello and de Cristofaro followed the outlines of Gambetti's designs, pricking the heavy paper at quarter-inch intervals with a spurlike perforating wheel for the long lines and a single-pointed pick for details. Then they glued each pattern to its proper place on the wall and, with cotton tufts that had been dipped into cans of powdered charcoal, patted along the perforated lines. When the paper was removed, the painting remained in outline on the wall. Di Bello chose the colors of tempera and with his steady brush went to work.

The angel with the veil and the angel with the inscription were positioned on each side of the back wall of the choir loft. Di Bello used the same technique for them as for the scenes downstairs, choosing golds and pinks in a limited range, with blue for the angels' wings and gray for the face on the cloth. On a scaffold high above the floor he painted the young twin angels, but not from the inspiration that Umbarger mothers imagined. Cattanei, intending a pleasant compliment, had asked in the presence of several children and parents: why don't we use these girls here as our models? The parents took him seriously, and later two of the girls came over to pose. Di Bello perched on the table in the basement, had the girls sit on a bench with their heads turned toward each other, and sketched their profiled heads. But when the time came to do the painting on the arch, he used Gambetti's perforated sketch, which was not based on a live model. He did the angel for the one side, then turned the paper over and made the same impression (reversed) on the opposite spandrel, and thus painted the second angel looking at herself across the arch. To Umbarger people, forty years afterward, the angels remained the two local girls and showed a resemblance to the models.

The murals of the *Visitation* on the east wall of the chancel and the *Annunciation* on the wall opposite it were the major works in paint, along with the big canvas of the *Assumption*, which was the last painted work. The three subjects were of Krukkert's choosing, all of them appropriate to a church named St. Mary's. The designs have stylized forms of human, angel, and dove, and the two scenes are set in Italian Renaissance tiled courtyards. The halos of Mary, Elizabeth, and Zacharias in the *Visitation* and of the angel in the *Annunciation* are of gold leaf, cemented to the wall.

In the background of both murals, much stylized but still recognizable, are the scenes that the artists saw when, taking a break, they stood outside the church and looked north. The *Visitation* has a green pasture, two symmetrical stands of ripe grain, and a cluster of farm buildings and trees—the Meinrad Hollenstein homesite. Far at the back of the *Annunciation,* behind another patch of grain and more pasture, beneath and a little to one side of the radiant dove that hovers over the meeting of Mary and the angel, is Jerry Skarke's house with its sheds and with the two big weeping willows in front. Di Bello, with his lifelong deference to age, rank, and ability, kept the Skarke homesite small, as Gambetti had sketched it; it does not show up even as clearly as the Hollenstein place. When he went outside, as he often did to stand for a few minutes and give his eyes a rest from the concentration on close-up details, he looked across the fields with a special awareness of which house was Jerry's.

Umbarger girls had been warned not to go into the church where the prisoners were working. Ormalene Brockman, who was sparkly, green-eyed, and fourteen years old, particularly worried John Coyle; he had seen the prisoners eyeing her. "Don't let her go in there alone," he told her mother, Mary Brockman. Though Coyle at other times guarded casually or not at all, he made a point of staying close when any of the girls were working. Ormalene came to work after school. The prisoners did not have a regular supper at the church but got cake, pie, and sandwiches and the like whenever they wanted during the afternoon. So she saw a good bit of them while she went about her chores. She developed a crush on Mario de Cristofaro, and they posed for a snapshot—the Neapolitan holding her hand and smiling at her, the schoolgirl giggling. De Cristofaro went over to the kitchen in the rectory more often than the other prisoners, partly because his duties as helper gave him more freedom than they had and partly because of his irrepressible sociability. He and Mary Brockman hit it off especially well. He snooped under pot lids, and sometimes he helped wash dishes.

Mathilda, the priest's housekeeper, was a fortyish, dowdy woman (Ormalene Artho remembers that she always smelled of Ben-Gay ointment) and a good-humored soul. One of the helpers during the project who particularly liked her was Evelyn Coyle. Evelyn went to St. Mary's several times during those weeks, by nonregulation means. She would leave the big house where she and her husband had a room and walk two blocks east and then eight blocks south on Main through downtown Hereford to the highway, where he would stop his truck and let her into the cab beside him. (No one remembers whether Di Bello stayed in front, too, or got in the back.) Evelyn enjoyed washing dishes in the rectory kitchen, as she enjoyed everything she did. She and Mathilda laughed the days away.

The Coyles never got caught in their shuttle operation, and they never worried about getting caught. They weren't worrying types, especially not Evelyn. In the evenings, on the way back to camp, John let her out at Main again, and she walked home.

In camp, the artists' fellow prisoners had their usual herring at mess. The artists thought of them after a day or two of the project and started filching pieces of chicken, slices of ham, bread, and whatever else they could easily conceal in their pockets to take inside the fence. Mary Brockman saw them. No doubt others did, too. Nobody said anything.

Mary was a pleasant-looking woman of thirty-eight, with short, waved hair. She was on the timid side and easily startled. She spent three or four days a week in the rectory kitchen during the project and probably got better acquainted with the artists, especially Di Bello and de Cristofaro, than any other Umbarger woman. To please Mario and the others, she gave them olive oil on their salad.

Once, Mary set out to make a special treat for the artists. She fixed spaghetti, using a sauce recipe that she went to some trouble to get from an Italian-American source. Mary Brockman followed the instructions as closely as she could. De Cristofaro had been snooping and sniffing, as usual, while she cooked, but she shooed him away, wanting the meal to be a surprise. When it was time, she carried the spaghetti and sauce over to the church in a big bowl belonging to Krukkert. Without saying anything she set it down in the middle of the table where the prisoners were waiting. When they saw what it was, the Italians let out such a yell of recognition and approval that she dropped the bowl the last inch or two. It gratified her to see how much the artists ate. Cattanei finally patted his little stomach and said, *"Basta!"*

The fact is that the big reception was an act. The prisoners' spy had told them what was cooking, and they set up the yell to please Mary Brockman. Di Bello says of the spaghetti, "They were awful." Maybe his allergy to garlic influenced him. But the prisoners did want to please the woman; the sentimental memories of the project have some foundation.

From the beginning of the project, the artists, and especially Di Bello, had a regular audience of one. He was a powerful man in overalls, unendingly curious about people and the world. The first time Paul Artho came in to watch, he announced that he was from a place near Di Bello's country and knew a word in his language. *"Porcamadonna,"* he said, and laughed. Di Bello laughed, too. "You are lucky because the church is disconsecrated," he said.

After that, Artho stood with his thumbs hooked in his overalls straps or sat on a wooden box at the base of Di Bello's scaffold. He smoked cigarettes (he always came with three or four packages, which he passed around), tapped the ashes on the littered floor, and talked with Di Bello. He told him how he had come to the states with only a suitcase and an umbrella and now had a good-sized farm with cattle. He asked if Di Bello's town was in the north of Italy—if it was, he would go and visit him if he ever made it to Switzerland. On a square page of Artho's little notebook, Di Bello drew him an outline map of Italy and marked on it Udine and the address, Via Roma 3.

Artho, who was fifty years old, asked about Di Bello's father and told about his own children. He talked on

and on, asked questions, listened attentively but sometimes anticipated the answers and phrased them
before Di Bello finished. Along with his curiosity he
showed a fatherly regard and consideration that Di
Bello found deeply touching. It had been a long time
since an older man had taken a real interest in him,
and in this setting he responded with more than ordinary warmth—far more than he had shown or felt in
his withdrawn state in camp.

Artho wanted to know about fascism and Mussolini. Why had Italy attacked Greece? Why had she
taken Ethiopia? He thought Mussolini had done
some good things for Italy. Did Di Bello agree? And
he thought Mussolini was not like Hitler. Di Bello
agreed, saying it had been a big mistake on
Mussolini's part to become an ally of Hitler, a mistake
even to have entered the war. Before the war, things
were good in Italy and there was no sign (so he said)
of anti-fascism. The mistakes started right after the
war in Ethiopia, when Mussolini began to think of himself as a military genius. But he had never been cruel
and barbarous like Hitler. Artho seemed glad of this
answer.

Di Bello had questions for him, too, about cowboys
and their duties, about cows and corn, and about
whether he owned a car and farm machinery. Conscious always of the proprieties, he avoided asking personal questions of a man twice his age. So he did not
learn the background of this crude and complex immigrant to whom he was becoming deeply attached.

Born in Switzerland, Artho left in 1914 at the age of nineteen and settled in the Umbarger community, where his sister, Paula Hollenstein, already lived. He worked as a butcher and as a farm and ranch hand before buying a farm in 1919. The same year, he married Louisa Skypala, "nothing but an angel in human form."

Artho owned one of the first motorcycles in the area, a Pope. Later, he bought a fine horse and rode it to Clovis, New Mexico, and back. All his life he wanted to see new places in new ways. He saw Umbarger barefoot; his feet developed rinds like smoked hams. When he was twenty-five, a neighbor watched him walk across a pasture full of goatheads—burs with spikes like carpet tacks. Artho stopped every now and then, said "Koddamn," brushed the stickers out, and went on. He would rest a foot on the fender of a tractor in the midafternoon sun of the hottest day. In Henry Bracht's shop once, the men talking with him smelled something burning. After a moment, Artho gave a jump. He had been standing on a coal.

He was a hard-working, thrifty farmer, narrowed to that life and to his Catholicism and yet restlessly curious about the world. He read murder mysteries, *Time* magazine, newspapers (some of them from Switzerland), and the history books his children brought home from school. On a small table in the living room he had a globe and a typewriter. He would spend hours typing letters to relatives and friends and mere acquaintances. His three sons serving in the Pacific sent him the name of every place they were stationed:

the first letter of every fifth word spelled it out. When a letter from APO San Francisco had the pages numbered I, II, III instead of 1, 2, 3, it contained a coded message, and after he worked out the name, Artho would rush to the living room to look for Bougainville or Okinawa or Pavuvu on the globe.

Artho was famously sociable, but he sought people out of curiosity as much as friendliness. When he drove his wife to Amarillo on their weekly trip to "take off the eggs," he sometimes sat and talked with the loafers on the benches around the courthouse while he waited for her. Later, he would tell everybody—his family, the meter-reader—everything the loafers had said. He would talk an hour about an hour's conversation.

By the mid 1940s, Artho was beginning to get a belly. He was short and so powerful he lifted the front end of a Model T truck while his sons put a block under it. He had short, reddish hair and a strong chin, and his blue eyes were remarkably sensitive in a man who hooked his thumbs in his overalls and strutted through the world belly-forward, staring this way and that.

Moonshining must have attracted him as a flouting, another way of going downtown barefoot. The law saw a difference, though. On March 9, 1927, the sheriff of Deaf Smith County went out to the Artho place with a search warrant. Artho, who was outside measuring oats, grabbed a couple of gallon jugs and broke them, but the sheriff salvaged enough of their contents to convince a jury. The sentence was one year in the Texas state penitentiary.[1]

Artho served much less than a year. His wife died on May 2 of the following year, at the age of twenty-nine,[2] after the Caesarian birth of their fifth child, Irene. He had delivered some of the other children himself, and the Department of Corrections had given him a furlough to attend this birth. There were problems that required the doctor in Hereford and the operation. After Louisa's death, Artho was given what amounted to permanent clemency by Governor Dan Moody on the recommendation of the Board of Pardon Advisers, of the physician who attended Mrs. Artho, and of "a number of the county officials and several hundred citizens," who said that "Artho is a first class German citizen, honest in every respect and industrious," and that "his young children need his further care and attention."[3]

A few months later, Artho typed a letter in German to his mother and stepfather in Switzerland. He had not seen them since going overseas. He said his children were healthy and thriving and that there had been sufficient moisture for his crops.

> You want to know what I expect to do, well I don't know
> that myself yet, I will just let the wagon roll until it ends
> up somewhere, the dear Lord will add something of his
> own. It seems to me very often that human life with all
> that goes with it is already laid out for a person when he
> first sees the light of the world. But why my so dearly
> beloved spouse was called away is still an unanswered rid-
> dle to me today . . . I feel sometimes as if God had torn
> my heart from my body I could cry out from sheer woe,
> but what good would it do? . . . I am sitting here in com-
> fort and should not have to worry about anything. I have

enough of everything, but the blow has hit me too hard . . .
But I hardly think you understand me, you never saw or
knew her, in short She was nothing but an angel in
human form.

The Artho children were motherless, and work
would keep their father in the fields for most of every
year. He found a wife, Mary Roeder, at High Hill—a
German community 550 miles to the southeast, near
Schulenburg, Texas, that had contributed Friemels,
Skarkes, and Skypalas to Umbarger. She bore him
seven children.

During the Depression, the Artho boys followed
jackrabbit drives to pick up the carcasses that the
hunters had discarded after cutting off the ears for the
penny bounty. Some of the rabbits, the Arthos ate;
some they fed to the hogs. In 1933, Artho bought a
1929 Pontiac for forty dollars but couldn't pay for it; it
was repossessed. But in 1934 he drilled an irrigation
well, one of the first in the area, powering it with a
belt drive from a Model D John Deere tractor.
Electricity came in 1937. Though Artho's bank
balance at one time that year was $23.54, he bought a
car early the next year, a black 1935 Ford V-8 coupe,
and wrote a $250 check for it.

For thirty-one years he did not try to go to Switzerland. He had not gotten an extension of his permission to delay the beginning of his military service, and
he was afraid that even though he was a naturalized
United States citizen, the Swiss would arrest him if he
returned.

During the project at the church, others came to watch the artists from time to time, though none returned day after day as Artho did. One farmer proposed that Cattanei make a ring for him like the one the prisoner was wearing. The artist agreed but said the farmer would have to give him a fifty-cent piece from which to make it. That was one of the two or three occasions when a guard other than John Coyle was with the prisoners. The guard was a stocky, surly fellow. "No," he told the farmer, "you can't have that done. Just let him alone." A prisoner would keep the coin and make the ring of something else, the guard said. Di Bello practically snorted when reminded about this exchange, thirty-seven years afterward. Cattanei steal a coin! But the guard's attitude seemed to the prisoners to be that of a typical *caman*.

Of course Father Krukkert came in a couple of times a day to see how work was going. He lay awake nights worrying that the project would not be finished, and for a while he thought the artists were dawdling to string it out. If they were, they stopped when the word came that they were to be repatriated within a few weeks. They did want to finish their work, and Krukkert wanted to dedicate it on December 8, the Feast of the Immaculate Conception.

Sometimes one or two of the prisoners walked over to the school to talk to the children about Italy or to sing. ("Don't Fence Me In" was a favorite of the prisoners.) Di Bello went three or four times. The last time was near the end of the project, when the Christmas holidays were approaching. The children in the room for lower grades asked Di Bello to draw Santa Claus and his reindeer on the board. He did so with colored chalks, astonishing the children by answering their questions over his shoulder as he drew. What did people eat in Italy at Christmas? Did children get presents? Di Bello, who drew the picture from Santa Clauses he had seen in *The Saturday Evening Post* and *Time*, told the kids that in the north of Italy the stockings were normally hung up on the night of January 12 and opened the next morning to see what Santa Lucia had brought. But in his family, because of his father's origins, the bringer, as in southern Italy, was Befana, a personification of Epiphany, who came on the night of January 6. There was a *creche* in the living room, and he and Bruno laid their stockings nearby on the floor or a chair. During the night, the wrinkled old woman, carrying a pack, came down the chimney to leave toy cars, balls, and Perugina chocolates. For naughty children she left pieces of coal.

The Umbarger children liked the drawing so much that they decided to leave it on the board till after Christmas. They sent a letter on a piece of tablet paper to Di Bello at the church, thanking him. "Every one in the room said that Santa and the reindeer looked as if they were alive," the letter said. "We shall always remember you and the other Prisoners of War, Always your friends." It was signed by twenty-three children bearing seventeen Umbarger surnames. Di Bello was touched by the letter, and of course he kept it.

One teacher at the school, Sister Martina Eiber, said she esteemed Umbarger students above all she had taught elsewhere. But she disliked their treatment of strangers. It was not just the occasional Protestants, children of families that rarely stayed in Umbarger more than a few years, who suffered. It was bad also for a Catholic outsider like the boy named John who had been in Umbarger only since his mother, Mathilda, came to keep house in the rectory and to cook for Father Krukkert. Though three or four of the children played with John and invited him to their homes, most of them snubbed him. He had more against him than his newness. His classmates responded to the drop in the tone of their parents' voices without understanding the words. The facts were that the child's mother had no sign of a husband, and that she and her son bore the surname she had been born with thirty-nine years ago in Germany. There were generous exceptions among the children as among the old residents. But Krukkert's example, giving shelter to the whispered-about woman, did not persuade many.

Language was an element of Umbarger's apartness. All Umbarger people understood some German and most could speak some, though only the old ones preferred it to English. And the English, even that of the children, sounded different from general West Texas. The influences conflicted, and still do. Some people pronounced Ben Koch's name as Kotch, some as Cook (his own pronunciation), and some with the German sound of the *ch*. Some said Oombarger; most made the first syllable rhyme with "hum." More than forty years after the St. Mary's project, and long after the practice of threshing grain was outmoded, some people still call it "trashing." Young people who don't speak German are likely to say "I vas" and to throw an "already" into a sentence. And most Umbarger people have a name for the non-German, non-Catholic settlers around them, many of whose ancestors came from South Texas and, earlier, Arkansas and the southern Appalachians. They call them Yankees.

In 1945 as now, St. Mary's Church brought Umbarger people together at times other than mass. Children attended catechism and mass in the basement of the church for an hour every morning before class (it was a state-supported school, but the Sisters of Mercy supplied the teachers.) Dances and cakewalks were held in the old frame church, which is no longer standing. Priests came from all around to participate in forty-hour devotionals.

Services were rather plain, and until the transformation of the last part of 1945, the interior of the church made them seem more so. But Krukkert wanted everything about the services and their trappings to be just so. Amalia Bracht carefully washed his vestments, the linens for the altars, and the long cloth for the communion rail. Mary Brockman ironed them. She lived just across a dirt street from the elevator, on the south side of the tracks. If the vestment was a little crushed by the time she got to the church with it, Krukkert would grumble something like, "Well, Mary, dot's not right," and try to pat out the wrinkles. Mary, who is not tall, would reply, "I just wouldn't care to have to walk over the track and all the way over here holding it in the air," and he would laugh at that.

For communion, Krukkert used an Angelina golden muscatel, eighteen percent alcohol, which he stored in its barrel in the basement. In those days before Vatican II, only the priest took the wine at communion. Krukkert put a wafer into the mouth of each communicant during the ceremony, which was held in the basement in the weeks of the project. He prayed that through this ritual the body of God would convey each soul to eternal life.

T W E L V E

If Di Bello could have seen through the walls of Jerry
Skarke's house—the one that showed in the *Annunciation*—the life of the girl with the pretty legs and the
pert smile would have touched him and yet have
seemed thoroughly strange. A typical resident of the
Texas Panhandle would have found it nearly as
strange.

Jerry had seen little of the outer world. She had
quit high school after her first year, as so many Umbarger children did, having work to do at home and
having picked up more knowledge of the world than
they expected to need inside the wall of Umbarger's
separateness. She went to Amarillo for a while, to
drive a delivery truck for a food store that had lost her
male predecessor to the service, and to study singing
at the Musical Arts Conservatory. The voice training
made her a better singer at St. Mary's later on, but she
wanted to sing popular music, not classical, and she
quit taking lessons. She quit work, too, and went
home after four months at the store and four with the
telephone company.

She had never been interested in travel. Even Amarillo, a town of only 65,000 then and only twenty-nine miles from Umbarger, seemed big and violent. On the night of April 6, 1944, she and two or three other girls went to the Double Dip at the south fringe of downtown Amarillo. They had refreshments and then got into line to pay—the place was full, though it was a Thursday. A tall man dressed in black strode in by way of the corner door. A small middle-aged woman, coming from somewhere inside, pushed Jerry out of the way and hurried behind the cashier's stand. The man reached in front of Jerry with a revolver in his hand and shot four times. The woman's body jerked upward and fell. Four men disarmed the killer, who, it developed, had been served with divorce papers that afternoon. His daughter, who had been in a booth with her mother and was about Jerry's age, ran back and forth, screaming.

"I'd rather drive the truck in the harvest," Jerry told her mother, and she left Amarillo.

Jerry Skarke Gerber lives in Umbarger now, only a block or so from St. Mary's. But during the war the Skarkes lived a quarter-mile north of the church, across flat fields. Jerry was the eldest of five children. She, her sister, Lucy Ann, and their mother, Marie (a beautiful, dark-haired Wisconsin woman, full-lipped and blue-eyed), did most of the work at home and most of that on their 160-acre farm. Otto Skarke, father and husband, had a full-time job at the Farmers Elevator. Still, other Umbarger men with jobs kept their wives from having to do men's work such as driving tractors or hauling hogs to market in four-wheeled trailers.

"Are you a widow woman?" people in Amarillo asked Marie Skarke, seeing her with her load of hogs.

Marie, with the help of the older girls, put an eleven hundred-paling fence around the garden and part of the yard. They cut the palings, gave them two coats of white paint, sank postholes by hand in the hard red-brown soil, and set the palings in a perfect line. More than once, Marie lay exhausted on the ground between the palings and wept. She got up afterward and went on with the work. "I wanted a purty fence," she explained.

Jerry and Ann slept in the northwest bedroom, which had flowered wallpaper that their mother had put up using home-cooked starch glue, as she had done in every room of the house. On the wall were side-by-side paintings of the Sacred Heart of Jesus and the Sacred Heart of Mary. Another picture showed a boy and a girl walking across a bridge over a stream, with an angel hovering protectively over them. Outside the girls' room at night, the windmill turned in the wind, its sucker rod making a peaceful, reverberant clank—another sort of guardian angel.

With the same obedience that she rendered to her parents, Jerry went without fail to mass. The thought of not doing so never seriously occurred to her, even when she lived in Amarillo out of sight of her friends and family and could have slept late on a Sunday without anybody's finding out. Like John Coyle, she believed in a literal transubstantiation.

Between six and six-thirty in the morning, Otto Skarke got the girls up. He was rather quiet, a bald man with a narrow, curved nose. Jerry dressed by the kerosene stove in the dining room if it was chilly. She put on jeans, pulled four-buckle overshoes over her oxfords, covered her thick brown hair with a scarf, and went out to the shed. There, by lantern light, she milked the four or five Guernseys and Jerseys that were fresh at a given time. Then she poured the foaming milk into the separator tank and turned the crank to separate the milk from the cream. After every use she took the separator apart and washed it in hot, soapy water. The Skarkes took the cream in five-gallon cans to sell at the creamery in Amarillo once a week. They also took eggs and sometimes calves. Jerry tells about those hard days without seeming bitter. She gives the impression that she works as hard now as she did then.

When eggs cracked, they could not be sold. The Skarkes *had* to eat them. Mrs. Skarke made, among other things, angel food cakes with the whites and yellow cakes with the yolks. The family had little money but plenty of food. There was home-churned butter, an especially deep gold if it came from the Jerseys. There were homemade jellies and jams, often of plums and cherries from the family orchard; tomato preserves; and orange marmalade. The marmalade was too bitter for Jerry. She did not like cracklings or other greasy things, either.

She had skittish tastes in things other than food. She learned to play the steel guitar, but only to please her friends; she did not like the twangy sound. She had an adolescent girl's squeamishness, the reflection of an innocence that had only begun to notice shadows. Until she was sixteen years old and heard a sermon by a visiting priest, she had not really believed in an evil force in the world. At seventeen and eighteen (though magazines and movies were full of pictures of soldiers watching girls in short skirts and though she felt herself in love with Ray Gerber, a Seabee from the neighboring town of Nazareth) she had no notion of how her own pretty legs, her heavy, soft hair, her straight carriage, and her smile affected men. She did not know what a crucible deprivation was for the desires of soldiers and for the Italian prisoners of war who had shocked feed on her family farm.

The "wall" did shelter Umbarger girls, but from only certain realities. It is hard to help raise and butcher thousands of fryers, as Jerry Skarke did, and still think life altogether beautiful and death dignified. Using a metal blade, Jerry scraped the chicks' droppings into a tub to be put onto the fields and garden as fertilizer. She mixed a wet mash of clabber, salt, and ground maize or wheat that she fed the chicks. When she took it out to the chicken house, one or two skinned carcasses of jackrabbits, shot by her father, were often hanging there near ground level where the chickens could peck the red flesh off them.

On butchering days, Jerry and the others worked amid a stench of warm blood and feathers, cutting off heads, plucking carcasses, cleaning out abdominal cavities, and scraping entrails onto newspapers to be thrown into the field for fertilizer. The papers were not thrown out with them. The Skarkes never had a mess.

The school was almost as close to the Skarke house as the church was. Until she dropped out, Jerry worked at her lessons dutifully. Her high school teacher, Sister Martina Eiber, liked and admired Jerry and thought her a good student.

Late one afternoon in the fall of 1945, without any conscious agreement, a young woman 400 yards from her home and a young man 6,000 miles from his found themselves outside St. Mary's Church together. They were on the west side of the building. From most directions, a human figure (or two figures) could be seen from a quarter-mile and more; the few leafless elms around the church offered no conceal-ment. At any moment, Krukkert or another of the prisoners might step out a door of the church or the rectory, a farmer-trustee might show up in his truck, or a child might come running and skipping out of school. Talk would take time. What could they say to each other, anyway?—"If it weren't for the ocean?" "If I weren't a POW?" "If it weren't for Ray?" Anything without the qualifying clause would be a lie.

Di Bello had not stood so close to a girl in over three years. The calls back and forth between him on his scaffold and the girl with the smile that squeezed up her eyes and arched her eyebrows had been as stimulating as extended hands that couldn't quite touch. He took her in his arms and kissed her. That was all. Soon the working day was over and Di Bello rode back to camp, where he performed a mind-closing of the kind he had invoked against various other impossibilities. But Jerry Skarke, for whom even Amarillo was too far from home, lay awake a long time that night, moved as never before.

Geraldine Skarke Gerber

THIRTEEN

At the Hereford camp a shakedown inspection in the officers' compound seventeen days after the beginning of the Umbarger project caused an outburst of complaints. The inspection started at two p.m., and prisoners were kept in the mess halls after lunch (such as it was). The purpose of the inspection seemed to be primarily to find articles of clothing not properly stamped *PW*. After sixty-five American soldiers had gone through the barracks in the absence of the occupants (except that each soldier was paired with a POW officer who acted as an observer), the prisoners were assembled in the company street and searched.[1] By then the sun was fairly low; the temperature was near fifty degrees, and there was a west wind.[2]

Eleven prisoners submitted written complaints afterward that officers were made to stand for a long time in only their underclothes as their outer clothing was taken away to be restenciled. Some said the searchers called them names. Several said they were pushed. Of course the indignity and the roughness (to whatever extent they actually occurred) were more

strongly felt by the Italians, or at least more vociferous-
ly protested, than would likely have been the case with
Americans. The search in the barracks caused
protests, too. "After the inspection," a major said, "the
rooms were reduced in a way that we had the impression of a Vandals raid."

Di Bello characteristically had a more moderate
reaction. He wrote in his journal that when he
returned from Umbarger that evening he found that a
"special" and "physical" search had been conducted;
his own bed was unmade, and his wardrobe was in "a
certain disorder." But the major made a connection
between the search and *la fame,* saying he believed
that the inspection was an "effort to provoke incidents
tending to justify the harsh treatment of the last
months as a disciplinary action."

The American officer in charge of the shakedown,
First Lieutenant Stanley V. Deal, conceded that some
of the complaints were true; he said his men "were ordered to stop calling the prisoners 'sons of bitches,'
'bastards,' and 'slaves' just as soon as I overheard
these remarks." The "resentment and noncoopera-
tion" of the Italians had made the guards angry, he
said. Deal said he saw no prisoner "pushed roughly
around" but agreed that an undershirt had been
taken by force from a certain officer, who he said was
"very arrogant" and had disobeyed the searcher.
Nobody had to stand for a long time in his underwear,
Deal said, because other prisoners always shared their
own outer clothing with the stripped ones.

An Italian lieutenant, paired with a searcher, refused to obey an American enlisted man's order to take a box of confiscated clothing to the supply room. Deal gave the same order and, being refused, told the prisoner to go to the compound office and wait for him.

> In the office I questioned him about his refusal to obey orders, he leaned on my desk, then I ordered him to stand at attention. I told him that I'd have to punish him and was about to have a confinement order typed out, when I recognized him as the Prison of War who had complained previously of losing weight so rapidly that he believed he was going to die. That the food was insufficient and in order to receive proper vitamins for his upkeep & health he had to eat grasshoppers, crickets, worms and rattlesnakes, after careful consideration off the above, I explained that he should get a haircut and restencil his clothes which had faded markings. He was then dismissed.

What saved the Italian from the guardhouse, pretty clearly, was an officer's queasiness about rocked boats.

Although acknowledging the accuracy of some of the complaints, Deal said he had also noticed that the searchers paired with English-speaking prisoners for the search "were conversing as they walked from building to building, in some instances, the american searchers gave the PW's cigarettes when they lit one for themselves." He said the prisoners' complaints "point out the ugly incidents, but give no hint to many of the good things our American soldiers are accustomed to and did do on this day." The same could be said of the similar complaints throughout the life of the camp. The Americans' responses seem to have been just as one-sided.

| • |

One of the branches of the Hereford POW camp was established at Dumas, north across the South Canadian River from Amarillo, where workers were badly needed for the American Zinc Company smelter. Sixty prisoners were sent to work there.[3] Before they arrived, a six-page packet of instructions was given to supervisors at the plant. It warned them that the prisoners would be "in no way like the civilian employees you have been working with," for "they are on the other side and do not believe in us or anything we are trying to accomplish."

> In addition . . . , there is a big difference in their way of thinking and ours. They have been taught from earliest childhood that such traits as kindness, patience, and sympathy are weaknesses of character—not qualities to be appreciated, but to be despised and taken advantage of whenever possible. In view of this fact, it is up to you to be firm, exacting, and impersonal with the POW's at all times. It is the only way you can have their respect.[4]

The supervisors were told, "When these prisoners are repatriated and get back to their own country, they will, if they have not been held to strict accountability, describe us to their countrymen as being a weak and coddling people."

FOURTEEN

The works at St. Mary's were carried out with more
and more awareness of the approaching deadline.
The biggest project, the oil-on-canvas of the assumption of Mary into heaven, came last. Cattanei, Gambetti, and, to a lesser degree, Di Bello, joined in that
project, which took seven to ten days to complete.
The painting was after Titian and was influenced by
Murillo's *Immaculate Conception.* The medium per-
mitted richer colors and a more fluid treatment than
had been possible in the tempera murals.

The carving of the *Last Supper* took shape slowly,
and Carlo Sanvito, toward the last, took it to camp
with him in the evening so he could keep on working.
(The two noncoms had also to carve the oaken planks
into reliefs of wheat and grapes for the trim around
the altar.) In the *Last Supper,* not all the figures of the
disciples are in quite the same postures as in the Da
Vinci painting, and Christ's countenance is turned
more to the front than in the original. Maybe the
grain of the wood dictated the changes. Naturally the
tension in the carving is less than that in the painting,

and partly for this reason, the wooden cups, plates, and decanter seem especially prominent. So the setting is more emphatically a supper, appropriate to Father Krukkert's partaking of the consecrated wine and his distribution of the Host.

John Coyle, restless, was in and out of the church. He watched the carvers sometimes; it was fascinating to see the figures of Christ and the disciples come alive and to see the shaping of the meal that had become the center of the Catholic ritual. He spent some time in the kitchen of the rectory, too, visiting with Evelyn and Mathilda. The housekeeper, who had no sense of style and who could not afford nice clothes anyway, found it intriguing that he had knitted stockings for a living in civilian life. She talked and kidded with him in her old-country tones. A lot of the time, Coyle simply walked around outside. Given his justifiable certainty that the prisoners didn't need guarding, there was not much for him to do around the church. He enjoyed talking with Di Bello on the trips to and from the work site, and the prisoners, feeling more and more relaxed as they got deeper into the project, developed a routine of spelling his name aloud in unison with him when he stopped at the gate on the way out. "C-O-Y-L-E," they shouted, startling the guard.

Kids seldom came to the church while the artists were at work. They were in school most of the working day (though the work went on on Saturdays, too), and their parents had discouraged them from hanging around. John, the son of Krukkert's housekeeper, lived in the basement of the rectory (his mother had a room upstairs, next to the kitchen), and when he had his homework finished the priest would let him go and play. This was the unhappy little boy whom most of the others shunned because he was new and did not have a father. Sometimes Coyle would tell him about major league baseball teams or get out on the parking lot with him and kick a football around.

The Coyles took to West Texas easily enough; John liked the flatness, which reminded him of the Zane Grey books he had read as a child. He and Evelyn, with another couple who had a room in the same house in Hereford, rented a car once and went on an outing to Palo Duro Canyon, a colorful gorge that appears without warning in the plains south of Amarillo. They went to Carlsbad Caverns in New Mexico, too, and sometimes to Amarillo for shopping.[1] West Texas was certainly different from his Pennsylvania home, but John (and Evelyn) looked for things and people to like, not dislike. He came from Easton, a dozen miles downstream from the foundries of Bethlehem. It was a country of hills, streams, and forests—features that scarcely existed in the Texas Panhandle.

Coyle was called up in September 1941 but his doctor, a member of the draft board, deferred him until he could try to gain weight under the doctor's regimen. He was five-feet-eleven, weighed 125 pounds, and had a twenty-six inch waist. In November, he finally got a knitting machine at Chipman Knitting Mills, after ten years of working there as a helper for ten to fifteen dollars a week and waiting for an opening as a knitter. He made eighty dollars a week on the machine and felt so rich he bought a Chevrolet Master Deluxe for $800. When the attack on Pearl Harbor was announced, he was sitting in Evelyn Border's house on Front Street, six doors from his house (her father had built the Border house, as Coyle's maternal grandfather had built his, narrow, straight-sided, and frame); he was reading the Sunday funnies and waiting for Evelyn to come downstairs. He heard the news on the radio and thought what fools the Japanese were.

"In a couple of months," he said to himself, "they're going to get it."

A few months later, having gained ten pounds, he was drafted. He left home on May 9, a month before he and Evelyn had planned to be married. At the induction center at New Cumberland, Pennsylvania, he found no shoes that fit. He wore size 12AA; his feet would not spread out to fill the narrowest shoes available even when the noncom in charge of the fitting made him stand on one foot. So the noncom got a bucket of sand. "Now, stand on one foot and hold this," he said. The shoes were still too wide. After thirty days, some of the right size arrived.

Coyle was sent to Miami Beach, Florida, for basic training, and from there to Sioux Falls, South Dakota, where he helped open an Army Air Corps installation to train radio operators. That winter he caught pneumonia and spent thirty days in the hospital. He went home on the train to recuperate, the hard seatbacks hurting his sore lungs. The next winter he married

Evelyn while on a six-day leave. Because she was Lutheran, the wedding was not in St. James Catholic Church but in the parsonage. They agreed to raise their children as Catholics. Both families had doubts about the marriage on religious grounds. Not Evelyn.

"Everybody mind their own business and leave us handle it, and we'll make out," she said.

She joined her husband at Hereford a few weeks after his arrival in April 1945. They rented a room upstairs in a house at the west edge of town, owned by a farmer who kept chickens and rabbits in the yard. When John was home, he and Evelyn sunned themselves on the southwest balcony, up among the elm leaves, or played catch with a softball in the yard; if one of them dropped the ball, it came up armed with goatheads. Coyle took long walks along the dirt roads west of the house. His wife kept busy at the USO, taking a crafts class designed to help wives of servicemen avoid boredom. She had always been good with her hands and unable to keep them still, and she made more jewelry than any of the other women. She and John were surprised at the West Texas dust which came up in clouds in the springtime ("What is that there, that big yellow sky?" he asked the first time) and seeped under the windows to make a thick layer on the sills. But they liked the cloudless weather, a nice contrast to the damps and glooms of the East. Evelyn knew nothing about the dangerous part of his job at the camp—he usually kept quiet about worrisome things. She wouldn't have worried much anyway. It wasn't her nature.

The dangerous part of Coyle's job was an after-math of the fatal stabbing of the Italian corporal. Every evening after supper, armed soldiers in a jeep would take Coyle to the gate of a compound and let him out. He would walk deep into the compound, alone and unarmed—otherwise, prisoners might seize his weapon—to count knives in the mess halls. "It gave me an eerie feeling," Coyle said. He would hear not a sound, except possibly prisoners talking inside the barracks he passed. On a warm evening, prisoners would be sitting on the steps. They would look at him and not speak. Sometimes, he said in a letter, "the hair raised on the back of my neck, knowing I was being watched every step. remember these people were locked up for years and at any given moment one of them might go berserk, and more than once it happened in that camp." In the mess halls, the knives were kept in a case on the wall, each knife in its own slot. If there was an empty slot among the dozen spaces, a knife was missing. That would mean a tense situation—prisoners made to form in the company street while the guards thoroughly searched them and the barracks. But Coyle never found an empty slot. He counted while the Italian mess sergeant stood silently by. Then they locked the case, and he went on to the next mess hall.

The job was more interesting, at least, than his work had been before he got a machine at Chipman's. His first job, after he completed the eighth grade, "graduating" second in a class of three boys and five girls at St. James, was as a bicycle-riding delivery boy for Western Union. After six months, he got a $7.20-a-week job winding cord onto wooden shafts in a factory that made conveyor belts. The thunder of the looms shook the building. Coyle worked a forty-hour week in four days, on Fridays going to continuation school, as the law required: "You didn't learn anything."

The next year, when he was fifteen, he went to work at Chipman's, where his mother had been employed since her husband's death six years earlier. (He had been a night-shift worker; Coyle would say later that he had never known his father.) He worked nights, on ten-hour hitches until Roosevelt and the eight-hour day came along, and took a sack lunch for his fifteen-minute lunch period. Standing on a wooden walk over the concrete floor, he helped two knitters, meanwhile learning, over a period of years, the operation of their intricate machines. Nobody would quit a job as a knitter in those hard times. When Coyle finally got his machine, it was because Chipman's had decided to put on a second shift. His work and his mother's made it possible for his brother, who was five years younger, to go through high school. But John did not feel martyred, he says, and did not mind leaving school. It was a time when boys did that, if they were lucky enough to get a job.

Girls did, too. Evelyn went to work at fourteen for the same belt factory as John. In the early 1930s, she, too, went to Chipman's, where her deft fingers got her a job as a topper, preparing the tops of men's socks for knitters, taking home about twenty-five dollars a week. She bought a seal coat for fifty-nine dollars.

Later she became a wet-legger, putting knee-length socks onto forms for pressing, on a two-to-ten shift. After work she would walk to a rink on 20th Street, skate till 11:15 and walk home.

John and Evelyn started dating when both were eighteen or nineteen. They would meet at Bushkill Park and go roller skating. Then he would walk her home. She was a good skater. He, with his long feet, wasn't graceful, but he didn't fall. He was wiry and athletic, a good fastball pitcher for the Easton Earls, a semiprofessional team so-called—the players got no money. Evelyn was attracted by his scrubbed neatness, and although he never pushed a conversation along, she enjoyed his quick, droll comments. They went to baseball games, went bowling, swam in Lake Wallenpaupack in the Poconos, sometimes drove to Atlantic City to hear Sammy Kaye's or Tommy Dorsey's orchestra on a Saturday night, returning home after midnight. John could hear one or two notes of a record and identify the band or the singer. He and Evelyn did things together, as opposed to discussing things. Though he always read the papers—he would walk miles to get a paper—he wasn't one for talking out the problems of the world. On dates he was polite, but not to the extent of walking around the front of the car to let Evelyn out. She would not have been able to sit idle that long, anyway.

When he was called into the service, John was still living at home with his mother. Family had always been close to him, literally close, space being short in the Coyle house. He shared an upstairs bedroom with his mother, and shared the bed, too, until he was ten or eleven, since the room barely had space for the one bed. His mother's mother had another room, and his brother and uncle shared another. John's Aunt Nell lived next door and his Aunt Nora (both the Coyles and the Dundons were solid Irish) lived on the other side of her—three sisters in a row.

After he became eligible for a hunting license, at sixteen, John got a double-barreled L.C. Smith shotgun that his father had left him and went hunting Eastern cottontail rabbits in the hills and thickets around Nazareth, a few miles away. When he had a successful hunt, his mother made rabbit pie. At school, as long as he was in school, he behaved well—the nuns at St. James gave him no choice, he said—and made good grades, especially in history and geography. It was a mile to school, the Coyles' area not being Catholic except for their own little neighborhood. About his Protestant acquaintances, John thought, "They had their own religion. They thought as much of theirs as I did of mine." In his church he was told that the wine and wafers were changed into the blood and body of Christ, and he believed this implicitly. "If you don't," he said, "you might as well not go there."

Coyle took his mother and a friend of hers to Florida for a month in 1937, driving the Model A Ford that his mother had bought from a junk yard three years before. In a cabin in North Miami Beach, a grease fire started on the kitchen stove where Coyle's mother was cooking. A black caretaker and gardener lived in a garage behind the place. Coyle had noticed that he would go to the back door of his employer's house to be handed his meals, which he would take back to his garage to eat, never going into the house. When the man saw the fire, he ran to the door and stood there, yelling advice. "He'd holler do this, do that," Coyle said, "but he wouldn't come in that door." That was his first experience of the Southern taboo of those days, and it shocked him.

When he was on a troop train going from Florida to South Dakota after basic training, the train stopped on a siding in a little Alabama town. A crowd of children, most of them black, had come to watch the train and look at the soldiers, and the train windows opened in a hurry. The soldiers were hungry. "Run over to that store and buy me something to eat—a candy bar or anything," they said, reaching a coin to the nearest boy. The boys shook their heads and tried to give the money back. When the soldiers insisted, they ran off. Soon they were back. "They won't let us in that store," they said. Coyle in general believed that differences among customs were inconsequential, but he could not abide this custom or any other that struck him as inhumane.

Before Evelyn joined him at Hereford, he returned to his barracks after a furlough home and brought along a bottle of Four Roses to share with his friends. He himself drank only a little to be sociable. It was night when he came in. He put the bottle into his footlocker and went to sleep. At five in the morning he woke up. Somebody was fumbling in the locker. In a moment he heard the visitor break the seal on the bottle, remove the top, and swallow with big glugs, not stopping to breathe. Coyle did not interrupt him. It had to be a certain poor fellow, the company drunk. There were plenty of misfits at the camp, especially late in the war, when former inmates of German prison camps and wounded or otherwise disabled men were sent there. Colonel Carvolth reported, "New personnel arriving at this camp have very little self-confidence and even less morale and even poorer discipline, due to neglect on the part of officers and non-commissioned officers who seem to forget that these men are eager to make good, but because of their physical handicaps have been unable to perform their maximum duties."[2] Other factors in poor morale, throughout the life of the camp, were the isolation and bleakness of the place. The soldiers not able to look for the good features in an alien and initially unattractive place took out their anger on the prisoners. To Coyle, that was an almost blasphemous response.

The fall that he spent largely at Umbarger had been a dry one, though not disastrously so. The grass looked good enough; November had had no measurable moisture, but the late summer had been wet.[3] Just the same, grass wasn't so bountiful but what a farmer or a farmer-rancher begrudged any unnecessary inroads on it. Jackrabbits were bad that year. It takes 128 jackrabbits to eat as much of a pasture as a cow does, but often there are as many as 400 jackrabbits to a section of land—a square mile. The loss, in effect, of three head of cattle from the carrying capacity of a section is not trivial. Meinrad Hollenstein, one of the thriftiest and most efficient of the Umbarger farmers, hated supporting a bunch of scrawny rabbits, good only for chicken feed. One day Coyle heard him grumbling to Mathilda to that effect. The complaint started him thinking.

Sergeant John Coyle in the early 1940s

FIFTEEN

When Coyle heard Meinrad Hollenstein's complaint about the damage that jackrabbits were causing to his fields, he offered a suggestion. Whether or not Hollenstein understood the whole purpose of the suggestion, nobody knows now. But he was an agreeable fellow, and he readily went along with the idea. So Coyle and he planned an operation that in a small way defied hunger at the Hereford POW camp. Hollenstein, born in Switzerland in 1881, was a small, thin man with a mustache, a quick mover and quick talker. He worked for the church more than almost anybody else did. He got up at five o'clock many Sunday mornings and walked across the fields to light the furnace in the basement for the eight o'clock mass. He was always making or repairing something for St. Mary's. He made the scaffolds on which Di Bello and the other Italians worked.

Not long after approaching Hollenstein with his idea, Coyle, holding a twelve-gauge shotgun borrowed from Father Krukkert, perched on the right front fender of the Hollenstein Model A and, with Hollenstein driving, set out across the fields around St. Mary's Church. Coyle soon caught the rhythm of relaxing into the bumps made by the bunches of tough brown grass, and his blue eyes watched right and left in the swath ahead. Hollenstein, wearing his usual cap, peered over the bucking hood. There were so many jackrabbits it was as if the sky had dropped them instead of rain. When one flushed, all legs and ears, gawky and more comical than a true rabbit and surprisingly big to have been concealed by such sparse vegetation, Hollenstein with his quick reactions stomped on the mechanical brakes so that the front bumper dipped sharply toward the ground. The jolt catapulted Coyle forward. He landed in shooting position, his knees and long springy feet taking up the shock, and blazed away.

It was altogether different from Coyle's hunts at home, looking for cottontails in the brush around Nazareth. Hunting from the car, he easily filled a bushel basket with the soft-furred carcasses. The two men did so a good many times. Coyle found these excursions unsettling in a way: the jackrabbits screamed when wounded, as he had never observed the eastern rabbits to do. Once he went on foot into the fields and shot a jackrabbit running all-out. Hit in the hindquarters, the rabbit tumbled and tumbled, screaming its human scream all the way. Nonetheless, Coyle enjoyed these hunts. There is a color photograph of him holding up two jackrabbits and grinning, a typical happy hunter.

After the hunts, the two men drove back with the carcasses heaped in a basket. Hollenstein nailed them by their pink ears to the wall of a shed to clean and skin them. He did this skillfully, as he did everything, cutting around the legs and peeling the skins off like stockings as Coyle watched. When Hollenstein had dressed the carcasses, Coyle took them to the church, and, at the end of the working day, passed them out among the prisoners. In the privacy of the covered truck bed, each prisoner tied one end of a length of twine around the hind legs of a lean-muscled carcass, attached the other end to his belt, dropped the rabbit into his loose-fitting trousers, and tied the carcass to the inside of his leg below the knee. After the first time, Di Bello asked to have the fur left on his rabbit, and he also wrapped it in cloth to keep the cold flesh from touching him. Constrained perhaps by the same feeling or simply by his considerable reserve, Cattanei did not take part in the jackrabbit plot. Gambetti also refrained, giving priority to a project of his own.

What the men were doing could obviously have gotten them into trouble. It could have cost Coyle his stripes, too, as he knew very well, since he was the shepherd of the group and could be held responsible. ("Well, I could live with that," he said. "I wasn't used to big paydays anyway.") It could also very well have meant the end of the project at St. Mary's, which, entirely apart from the possible frustration to the creative instincts of the prisoners, would have meant an end to the Umbarger meals. The jackrabbits, moreover, would provide only a small, fleeting supplement to the diet of a few men in camp. So Coyle and the artists took chances disproportionate to any material benefits the operation would likely confer.

In view of the recipients' real hunger, the material benefits had, even so, to be given the first rank; but surely the smell of cooking meat in the evenings produced the sense of a small victory as well. This flesh from beyond the fence had the taste of freedom in it. The various vehicles of its coming might have made material for irony or even for a furtively prayerful gratitude if the prisoners had had only normal appetites. They were too hungry for much of either emotion, but they did at least know that a *caman* had been responsible for their late, light suppers.

"It is true that the ways of Providence are infinite," Captain Mario De Dominicis said as he chewed his portion of a rabbit. "This time, for instance, it came through the barrel of a shotgun."

But that kind of remark was the exception, as Di Bello remembers. The prisoners ate until the bones were clean, buried the bones, and that was it. The rabbits were spitted and roasted over the coal stoves provided for each box. De Dominicis did the cooking in Di Bello's barracks. It took about half an hour for a rabbit, turned several times on the spit, to cook through. Then De Dominicis cut it into ten or twelve pieces with a pocketknife, and the little meal began. Actually, it was not much more than a reminiscence of a real meal. Di Bello tried just a taste once and thought the meat good. Manzoni, his roommate, had a portion on a couple of occasions. In Zoagli, as a child, he had eaten domestic rabbit regularly—many residents raised rabbits at home—and he enjoyed the meat from St. Mary's, wild taste and all.

To get the jackrabbits into camp, Coyle tried to wait to unload his prisoners until after he had already passed the guard hut, explaining to the guard that they had worked hard and were exhausted. Sometimes this worked, and sometimes the guard on duty was a friend and let him pass unquestioned. When searches did occur, they were not always thorough.

But the luck at the guard hut sometimes failed. Coyle would say, if he had to say anything, "Seven prisoners from Umbarger—five Compound 4, two Compound 2." An especially conscientious or hostile guard would make the prisoners jump down for a search. So Captain Gorlato once spent a night in the guardhouse, and one of the noncoms spent five days (which represented that much time lost from carving the *Last Supper*). Once, de Cristofaro was set free after two hours of confinement, and Di Bello got off with a severe scolding from Chaplain Ferreri, who extracted a promise from him not to repeat the offense. Colonel Carvolth said that one more infraction would mean the end of the project. The prisoners kept on smuggling and Coyle kept on supplying. After all, they were under the duress of hunger—other men's hunger. For some reason, Coyle was never punished.

Gambetti stayed out of the rabbit scheme because he had his clothes full of chocolates. He smuggled them regularly to Second Lieutenant Giovanni Migliarini, the pianist, who had quit practicing to conserve energy.

The chocolates, filled with coconut, were supplied by Umbarger people. Migliarini soon regained enough strength to get back to his piano. Gambetti was caught by the guards once. When Migliarini's parents got a letter from their son about the man who had helped him, they sent a gift to Gambetti's wife: twenty-two pounds of peanuts.

SIXTEEN

At last conditions at camp improved. Bishop
FitzSimon's letter to Congressman Worley had had its
effect. General Bryan, the Assistant Provost Marshal,
wrote to Worley that he had asked the Eighth Service
Command to make a "complete investigation of the allegations" in the bishop's letter.[1] And on October 30,
an inspecting team, with representatives of the U. S.
Department of State, the International Committee of
the Red Cross, and the Italian Embassy, arrived at
camp.[2] Most likely, the weighing was done in connection with that visit.

On November 6, the bishop wrote to Congressman
Paul J. Kilday, a member of the Committee on Military
Affairs who had taken a hand at Worley's request, "I
have been informed that a very rigid investigation has
taken place and I have reason to believe that a decided
improvement will result."[3] A few days later, FitzSimon
said he had heard, with pleasure, that his letter had
"created quite a stir." He said that Ferreri, in an interview with Red Cross and Army representatives, had
supported the bishop's statements and even "made

additional charges." And he said the Italian ambassador (Alberto Tarchiani) had eaten with the prisoners "and was served a meal equally as palatable as that which I pretended to enjoy in company with the Italian officers."[4] As yet, the bishop said, he had not heard of any augmentation of the prisoners' rations. The next day, though, on November 10, he reported better news. He had heard that the canteens had been reopened so that prisoners could buy extra food, though their regular rations had not been changed.[5] The extra food in the canteens consisted of pretzels and condensed milk. Prisoners bought cans of milk—there was a big supply—and opened and drank them on the spot. Some complained that the milk and pretzels bloated them. But at least there was finally enough nourishment available.[6]

Of course the Army was not going to admit that much of anything had been wrong in the first place. Captain Lyle T. Dawson of the Eighth Service Command made an inspection on November 16, six or seven days after the beginning of the improvement that FitzSimon had observed. The next day, he gave a report by telephone to a lieutenant colonel in Washington and then spoke to General Bryan. The general asked if the prisoners' canteen had been closed recently. Dawson said he would have to ask. In a moment he got back on the line: "Colonel Carvolth stated that it had not been closed and that it is open now."[7] Unless Bishop FitzSimon and a long string of Italian officers unanimously lied, this statement was no more than half true by the letter and was totally deceiving in its spirit.

Bryan asked to speak to Carvolth, and he opened with a reference to a meeting scheduled two days later in the office of Assistant Secretary of War John J. McCloy on complaints about the treatment of the prisoners.

> BRYAN: We're getting a little hot about your camp down there, but I don't want you to get worried because I am going to bat for you whole hog.

> CARVOLTH: There is one thing I want you to remember, and that is this: this camp is just a dumping ground for the whole United States. All I've got here is just the scrap from over there.

Some unproductive exchanges about food and the hospital followed, and then this:

> BRYAN: Now there is one other thing: they told me up here, and I didn't believe them—I'm frank with you— they said that they went to one meal down there and they didn't have any salt. Have you ever run out of salt?

> CARVOLTH: There have been complaints from time to time on salt. I took that up with my . . . [unintelligible] officer and they had required more salt from time to time. So they supplied more salt. . . . They said they were short on salt but my commissary officer didn't concur with that.

> BRYAN: In other words, your commissary officer said that you had as much salt as any American ration would use but that was not as much as an Italian ration would use?

To this mysteriously received perception on the part of the general, Carvolth replied, "That's right. However, we did supplement that, even."

There was talk about other complaints, which Carvolth said had been unjustified.

> BRYAN: Then in your opinion those people are just suffering from their own damn thoughts?

> CARVOLTH: That's right. Things are just what they make it down here.

> BRYAN: In other words, the morale question as you take it is generally just a pure Italian question.

> CARVOLTH: That's right.

> BRYAN: In other words, he just doesn't have the guts to get up and drive like a German.

> CARVOLTH: That's true. As I said before, they are our enemies, they are not friends of ours.

After a time, Dawson got back on the phone. About the Italian Major Cabitto's estimate of calories, he said, "I asked him where he got his authority for the calculations and he said he had a book there . . . of some kind of authority. I reminded the major that the Army diet of 2,500 was based on an Army calculation and the dispensing of the rations was of course done on that basis." It wouldn't do to use any outside authority, he told Cabitto. General Bryan approved of the response. "We use the regular U. S. Army calculations," he said. "That is settled."

Even though Carvolth had led Bryan (who was most willingly led) to believe that there had always been enough salt, Dawson himself said in the written report of his inspection that the soup, which he sampled, was lacking in salt; when told of this, as Dawson reported, Carvolth increased the salt ration by fifty percent. The inspection had been carried out the day before the telephone conversation.

Dawson reported further that canned milk "is sold in the canteens to the prisoners . . . and the prisoners are very pleased to get this." (No mention of the fact that they would have been pleased to have had it for the preceding six months.) He conceded that officers "do not indulge extensively in sports because they feel they do not have enough energy to expend on sports, because of their 2500 calorie diet." But working prisoners, having a more substantial diet, did play soccer and volleyball, he said. Dawson said he sampled the food in Compound 4 and found it "well prepared and palatable" (except for the saltless soup). The portions included soup, "a large three ounce mutton pattie by which part of the oleo, onions, lard, flour and potatoes were served" (apparently this meant three ounces *including* an unspecified amount of flour and potatoes), three tablespoons of soybeans, and a quarter-pound of bread. An increase of one-tenth of a pound of flour per man per week had been authorized on November 1 by the quartermaster in Fort Worth, and this had improved the diet, Dawson said. He said a spot check among prisoners in all compounds had revealed these facts:

(1) All said they would like more to eat.

(2) None would say he was in bad health and all said they felt good.

(3) None would say he was actually hungry except just before mealtime.

(4) All said they had lost weight since the reduced diet was adopted, but none thought they had lost weight within the last two months.

(5) Some said they felt better than when they were heavier.

This has an air of reasonableness. But in view of the other available reports, including those of prisoners, the question must be asked: just which prisoners did Dawson interview?

Dawson recommended that the market center at El Paso list substitutions of the same nutritional value for unavailable items on the daily menu, since the quartermaster at Hereford had "no means of calculating caloric or vitamin values." (Quite a discrepant statement from the one he had made to Major Cabitto—"that the Army diet of 2500 was based on an Army calculation and the dispensing of rations was of course done on that basis.") He also recommended that "2500 calories be furnished daily as a minimum to prevent lean days that have run as low as 2200 calories." He said, however, that the average daily caloric value of the food for each prisoner had been 2,623 in June, 2,450 in July, and 2,348 in August. (How did he know this, since the quartermaster at Hereford had no way of calculating caloric values and since substitutions apparently *had* been made at times?) Major Cabitto's estimates were not mentioned at all in Dawson's report. The report did say, however, that Cabitto's medical opinions had clashed with those of American doctors and that the major's complaints about these differences had caused "much discontent among the prisoners." Not any longer: Cabitto left camp on November 5 for repatriation,[8] twenty-four days ahead of the first prisoners to leave Hereford as a group for that purpose. It was a relatively pleasant way for the Army to silence dissent.

The November 19 conference in McCloy's office was ordered by Under Secretary of State Dean Acheson at the request of the Italian ambassador, Tarchiani. The ambassador said at the meeting, according to a summary of the proceedings, that "it is his opinion and that of the International Committee of the Red Cross that the situation at Hereford is not as it should be, that the prisoners are not treated according to the Geneva Convention, with particular reference to food. He said the prisoners were forced to eat potato peel pie. . . . These prisoners are noncooperative and the Ambassador has no special feeling for them, but he said they are not being treated as human beings . . . ." The Red Cross representative, Charles Huber, concurred. "He stated that, compared to the other camps he has visited, Hereford is worse than even German camps for American officers." McCloy said an investigation would be conducted, Bryan said one was already being conducted, and Tarchiani said that he "came to the meeting just to get assurances that such investigations would be made."[9]

A report to the Department of State from the Provost Marshal General's office on December 29 said "it is believed" that Huber's comparison could not be sustained. Of Carvolth, it said, "His administration of this camp has been as successful as could be expected under the trying circumstances."[10]

As to the character of the prisoners, Dawson found problems.[11] Officers and noncoms "constantly demonstrate their non-cooperativeness and actual animosity by violating Army Regulations and camp rules," he said. For example: they removed boards from the walks and made packing boxes and bedstands of them; they slouched and shuffled during headcounts and then snickered when they had thus confused the American officers making the counts; they kicked, pulled at, and cut the fences between compounds; they obstructed searches at the gate; most of them refused to give the American salute to American officers (the fascist salute had been out-lawed some months earlier[12]); and they feigned sleep or even hid under buildings at headcount time.

Dawson was told also that although Carvolth had al-lowed the prisoners to have a funeral with full military honors during the preceding month for a noncommis-sioned officer (who had died of natural causes), the speaker had "eulogized the deceased for approximate-ly two minutes and then spent from ten to fifteen minutes extolling the merits of the Fascisti." The prisoners, in short, were provocative, Dawson found, and yet they had never been punished beyond the limits of the Geneva Convention or Army regulations. In fact, "it is the studied opinion of the reporting of-ficer that the provocations offered and perpetrations committed by the prisoners of this camp are sufficient justification for even more severe punishment and that it should be applied to many more than those who have to this date received it. Further, it is his belief that the only reason more extensive and more severe punishment has not been given to the prisoners by the camp commander is his dislike for meting out any at all."

A letter essentially summarizing this report was sent to Congressman Worley in February by General Bryan.[13] It apparently constituted the *official* response to Bishop FitzSimon's letter.

Carvolth had support not only from his superiors but also, still, from FitzSimon, who in December said again that he believed that the American command at the camp had only carried out orders in cutting rations. "The responsible persons," he said, "are those who have incited the military authorities to adopt a rough treatment for these men, and I think that some of our high-powered radio commentators are to blame."[14]

A testimonial for Carvolth came from a representative of the War Prisoners' Aid Group of the Young Men's Christian Association. He said the commander had won the respect of the prisoners, who recognized his fairness and his "great desire to help them if they help themselves."[15] This was written at the end of 1944, before the reduction of rations. Also, for his work both at Hereford and previously at the German camp at Mexia, Carvolth was commended by the director of the POW division of the Eighth Service Command. The director said the colonel had doubled the output per man of prisoners working out-side camp and had re-educated Nazi prisoners with ex-cellent results, testified to in letters signed by many of the prisoners themselves.[16]

Hereford was both a tough camp to command and a tough one to be confined in, with constant hostility between prisoner and prisoner, between prisoner and guard. The Italians' zeal, whether essentially political or merely dutiful in inspiration, unquestionably turned obstructionist at times, just as some of the American guards sometimes showed insensitivity and even brutality. But Carvolth's own qualities of percep-tion helped him not at all. He considered the prisoners at Hereford to be of a "lower type mental-ly."[17] (The worlds of art and literature would be surprised to learn this.) Apparently the commander, during *la fame*, perceived the prisoners' physical state as dimly as he had seen their intellectual qualities. This was strange, because all he had to do was shift his gaze from orders and caloric charts to people. If he did know of the hunger, then his failure to act must be attributed to malice. In the absence of strong evidence that he knew, it is more reasonable to find him guilty of what his character does support: a cold, letter-of-the-law bullheadedness, nourished by his con-tempt for the prisoners under his command.

There can barely be doubt that the prisoners were inadequately fed during the months after V-E Day. The Army's report on the situation was based on an in-spection made after the worst conditions had been al-leviated and must, besides, be read with many reservations because of its self-serving nature. On the other side, the clerical witnesses—FitzSimon, Salvi, Fer-reri—had little (if anything) to gain by exaggeration, and John Coyle had nothing. But the strongest cor-roboration of their observation is in the fact that an American soldier and a party of prisoners thought it worth the chance of punishment and deprivation to smuggle the carcasses of wild animals into camp for prisoners to eat. The scheme had no value as propaganda: it was a secret, or so intended. And it gratified no political animosities on the part of John Coyle. He knew that men were hungry; he helped get food to them.

SEVENTEEN

The project at St. Mary's ended with the dedica-
tion at midmorning on December 8. Before the
ceremony began, the artists put a few last touches on
their work. Then the whole congregation, practically,
gathered in the sanctuary. (One absent Umbarger
resident was Otto Skarke, who seldom went anywhere
with his family; but Jerry and her mother were there.)
Bishop FitzSimon spoke. Krukkert and Ferreri took
part in the ceremony. Unfortunately, a strong west
wind was stirring up dust, but it was otherwise a clear
day[1] and the light gratifyingly showed off the nine
large and three small new stained-glass windows. They
had arrived from their manufacturer in Milwaukee
and had been installed by two enlisted prisoners—
Amedeo Maretto and Antonio Monetti—who brought
their skills to the project a couple of weeks before its
end. The names of Umbarger families were on the
windows as donors. Krukkert was happy with the windows and had come over to the church frequently to
watch the installation. Bishop FitzSimon addressed
some remarks in Italian to the artists and artisans, all

of whom sat on the front row. John Coyle sat with them. At the end, the bishop called on the whole party to stand and be recognized, but Coyle kept his seat. "*I* hadn't done anything," he explained.

People walked around and looked at the paintings, carvings, and windows. Next to the inner door at the back of the sanctuary, a bronze plate the size of a sheet of business stationery was fixed to the white plaster wall. It bore the names of the participants in the project and, underneath the names, a Latin inscription composed by Manzoni and rendered as follows by Di Bello: "Italian soldiers, prisoners in this total and dazzling new war, made this work to praise the glory of God and to reverence the memory of their unhappy, faraway Country."[2]

The prisoners, John Coyle, and the participating clergymen had lunch on big tables set up in the rectory in adjoining rooms with the separating glass doors opened. Mary Brockman, wearing a flowered summer dress, and Amalia Bracht prepared the meal; Mathilda, the housekeeper, was sick. Jerry and two other girls helped in the kitchen and later washed dishes. The prisoners filed past Mathilda's bed to tell her goodbye. She asked Coyle to remind one of them, in particular, to write to her when he got home, and Coyle tried his Italian for the purpose: "*Quando va arrivato in dentro li Italia, no dimenticar to scrivere to le donna.*" The prisoner laughed, waved, and said, "OK."

It was a big day for Krukkert; a sad one for the prisoners, who wept. Di Bello and de Cristofaro got Coyle's permission to go and see the Brockmans' house, a three-bedroom stucco next to the Farmers Elevator, of which George Brockman was manager. They wanted to be inside a real home, and though they had not seen a lot of George, they both (especially de Cristofaro) had become close to Mary. Since it was a day of holy obligation, George was not working, and he drove them home from church in his gray Oldsmobile. It was a pleasant house, with a rose trellis on the front porch. Inside, Mary gave them each a glass of orange soft drink, and her husband found on the radio the Metropolitan Opera broadcast of Verdi's *Un ballo in maschera,* which gave pleasure to their visitors—though less to Di Bello than the Brockmans imagined. On their tour of the house, the prisoners saw George Brockman's felt dress hat on a bed. That was bad luck, they said, and put it on a shelf. The visit lasted only about a half-hour, and after being assured that the Brockmans would answer their letters, the prisoners left with tears in their eyes.

Repatriation was supposed to come soon. The prisoners naturally hoped it would be before Christmas. One group from Hereford had left on November 29. But the dissenting countrymen, the ones who had collaborated with the Allies and joined Italian Service Units, got priority.[3] Then, before the end of December, a shortage of merchant seamen tied up more than 100 ships in ports all along the East Coast; now that the war was over, the seamen were taking the vacations they had had to put off. The shortage delayed not only the repatriation of prisoners but also the movement of U.S. occupational troops to stations in Europe.[4]

There was, at least, more food in camp than there had been at the start of the project, and Di Bello passed time, again, by painting. One of his projects was a portrait of John Coyle, for which he had the subject do several sittings in a barracks. (Gambetti gave Coyle a painting, too, an oil landscape set in the Rocky Mountains.) He waited for news of repatriation. He and de Cristofaro grumbled together about the delay of shipping: curse the Americans, they said, winning the war and then tying up the ships just as the prisoners were about to be sent home. Christmas dinner, at least, was better than the usual meal. With a $500 gift from the apostolic delegate in Washington, along with some other donated money, Father Salvi had augmented the holiday menu by buying 894 pounds of chicken, 23 pounds of turkey, 600 pounds of flour, 300 pounds of walnuts, 20 cases of Karo syrup, and $112.86 worth of candy and cigarettes.[5]

On December 15, Coyle got his orders for separation. He went to Camp Chaffee, Arkansas, along with other soldiers, none of whom had been expected. They all had to sleep on bare mattresses underneath their overcoats. After his discharge on the twentieth, Coyle went to St. Louis for the trip home, and found the first train full. He bought two sandwiches and leaned against the gate eight hours, waiting for the next train, which he was the first to board. *He* wanted to get home for Christmas, too. When he arrived in West Easton, there was a card for him from Mathilda.

"Boy is it cold here my my!" she wrote. She said she had seen a big jackrabbit run past the garden: "get your gun."

Two days early, Di Bello learned unofficially that he was about to leave for home. Then on January 18 he entered in his journal: "Official notice that the departure will be next Monday!!" The event itself rated capitals: "DEPARTURE FROM HEREFORD!" But before his train pulled out at 2:45 p.m., there was one more violent incident. With Di Bello in the group waiting to board was a lieutenant, Enrico Salerno, wearing a red beret with a blue tassel, the kind first awarded to the *bersaglieri* in the Crimean campaign of 1854. A guard noticed the color of the cap, shouted that the wearer was a bastard Communist, and ordered him to remove it. Salerno refused. The guard—or another guard—hit him on the head with his pistol and took the cap away. Salerno was treated at the hospital and returned to the train.[6]

Di Bello's group of 100 departing officers, including de Cristofaro and the writer, Giuseppe Berto, traveled through Gallup, New Mexico, and Flagstaff and Kingman, Arizona. Surveillance was light; they were allowed to open the windows. At Kingman, south of the tracks in a row that Di Bello judged to be at least twenty miles long, American planes back from Japan sat wing to wing waiting to be sold for scrap. Somebody estimated that there were 40,000. Di Bello remembered that Italians had fought the last year in North Africa "without a single goddamn bloody airplane protecting our flank." And Italy had entered the war against such a country! He and the other passengers went by train to near Los Angeles, were taken by bus to the port at Long Beach, and boarded a 17,000-ton Liberty ship, discordantly named for a fish: the S.S. *Marine Carp.* They waited on board for three days, 3,200 Italian prisoners in all. Then Di Bello wrote in his journal: "At 1330 we sail with very good weather and sea. Goodbye Bitter America *[Addio America Amara]!*"

Except for three seasick days in the Caribbean, it was a happy trip back for Di Bello until the approach and entry to Naples. Conditions were good. He was the interpreter for his group. The ship reached Naples on February 16. Three or four kilometers before docking, it was surrounded by hundreds of boats, their occupants not there to wave and cheer but to sell. They hawked pistols; blankets; fake passports; mattresses; uniforms ("This was very funny," Di Bello said) of every Allied and Axis nation; sisters of the boatmen; other girls; boys. On the pier, a ridiculous band of about a dozen pieces, its players clad in olive-drab Allied uniforms without insignia, played "stupid Neapolitan music"—*"Dove sta Za Za."* Two officers in the band saluted, but Di Bello and the others, not considering them representatives of their government, kept their hands at their sides.

In Naples, Di Bello stayed at de Cristofaro's house. On February 20, along with Berto and another *herefordiano* who had been a professor at the University of Venice, he left for home in a car whose driver made his living hauling rice, butter, and cheese to Naples and carrying passengers from Naples at exorbitant fares to the north of Italy. They spent the night in central Italy. The next day, Berto got off first at Mogliano Veneto—near the city whose destruction he had portrayed in *Il cielo e rosso.* The professor was next, and finally, at eight in the evening, Di Bello got home. Like the other *Nons*, he had a paper arrest of five days awaiting for not having collaborated. Supposedly he was to be confined to his residence except to go to work. But the arrest was never carried out.

By February 7, the rest of the prisoners had left Hereford.[7] There had been a flurry of excitement on January 24 when a tunnel—abandoned since V-E Day by its architect, a friend of Di Bello's—was discovered. The compound commander ordered it sealed with coal ashes.[8] When the camp closed, Colonel Carvolth was assigned as commander of the prisoner-of-war compounds at Fort Bliss, Texas, and before long he got another chance to show his attentiveness to regulations. On March 12 he reported to the post commander that the Army "K" ration issued to departing prisoners on trains supplied 3,600 calories, whereas nonworking prisoners of war were authorized only 2,300. Also, he said, the ration was nonregulation because of its value—ninety-nine cents a day, whereas American enlisted men accompanying the trains were authorized only seventy-five cents for subsistence. For future movements of prisoners, he asked permission to reduce the allowance per man to two-thirds of a "K" ration a day.[9]

In Umbarger, the transformed church was in use again by its parishioners. Servicemen came back, one by one, from overseas. Among them was Ray Gerber, a blond Seabee. He arrived in December, and he and Jerry Skarke soon began looking toward a summer wedding. Paul Artho, notified during December that his mother was seriously ill, went to New Orleans and tried to get aboard a ship to Europe, though he had no passport. Failing, he returned home and found a telegram saying she had died. On December 4 Father Krukkert signed papers carrying out a transaction he had begun during his vacation in September; he sold, for $19,000, the house at San Clemente.[10] He must have done so with comparatively few regrets, since he now had the successor to that project to compensate him.

It is unfortunate that when he was doing the murals in the church, Di Bello did not interpolate a jackrabbit or two into the Umbarger scenes in the background. Then the paintings, implicit records of talent and perhaps devotion imported from a prison camp, would have reflected also the uncomplicated kindness of John Coyle, who sent suppers of red meat back to the camp from the fields around St. Mary's.

EPILOGUE

In the four decades since its closing, the prison camp at Hereford has largely reverted to farmland. Prairie dogs have tunneled out a town where the compounds used to be. The water tower still stands, and various small ruins of buildings and foundations can be seen amid fields of castor beans and corn. The buildings were sold and moved soon after the war; many are in a community of dwellings for Mexican-American field workers outside town now, but a few have been converted into private houses in Hereford. The town has grown to a population of 15,000, mostly because of irrigation and good soil but in small part because of the soldiers from camp who married Hereford women and stayed. Umbarger has changed in less apparent ways. The civilians, soldiers, and priests who directly or otherwise influenced the lives of the St. Mary's artists and their fellow prisoners have aged and forgotten. Some have died, as have some of the artists. Among certain ex-prisoners, certain memories remain strong and are in fact *kept* alive. But for the others from camp and from Umbarger, small boxes of letters in the attic contain most of the detailed memories of events so long ago.

Colonel Carvolth, the camp commander during *la fame*, died in 1956, and his son, Joseph R. Carvolth, Jr., fifteen years later gave his papers from the Hereford camp to the Army Military History Institute at Carlisle Barracks, Pennsylvania. The collection contains documents that in effect accuse Carvolth of mistreating his prisoners: the bitter and imploring letters (including Berto's), the tables of before-and-after weights of the officers, a lieutenant's account of having shrewdly shown leniency toward a prisoner who had complained about the food. The only document in the Carvolth collection that tends to defend the collector is the report of Captain Dawson's inspection of November 1945. Since he preserved the documents, Carvolth must either have been dedicated to historical accuracy or somehow not have considered the contents derogatory to him.

John and Evelyn Coyle live in a neat house in West Easton, only a block and a half up the street from the house in which he grew up and three doors from the one in which he lived during their courting days. He retired in 1979 from a job operating a drill press for Bell & Howell; he had been with that company for most of the years since 1957 when Chipman Knitting Mills went out of business. He is slender and hard-muscled; he keeps in shape by doing 150 push-ups every other day and by swimming in a plastic pool in his backyard. Also, he walks four or five miles every morning. The walks go all around the pretty residential hills, but they always take him to St. James Catholic Church, where he stops and attends mass. He has missed Sunday services only twice in his life, and not once since 1945. But three of the four Coyle children, all of whom were brought up as Catholics (and all of whom live within twenty miles of their parents), have quit attending church.

Both the Coyles love the sun. They spend three months in Florida or Arizona every winter. To escape both snow and high taxes, John would like to move to some such place, but Evelyn does not want to leave the children and the twelve grandchildren. As always, she keeps her fingers busy cooking, sewing, quilting, and housecleaning. John has become a skilled and particular tinkerer and carpenter. He has given up one of his old diversions, though. After years of hunting buck deer in the Poconos, he finally killed one, more than twenty years ago. He wrote a letter about it: "When I seen that beautiful animal lying there with the blood pumping out of it, that was the end of my hunting days."

Of the many artists who were prisoners at the Hereford camp, the most widely known today is Alberto Burri, whose large works incorporate materials such as wood, steel, ceramics, and scorched polyvinyl. Some of his works were displayed in 1982 at the Brooklyn Museum and at the Museum of Modern Art in San Francisco. It was at the Hereford camp that Burri, a medical officer, decided to become an artist, and Dino Gambetti gave him much encouragement.

Burri was not of the St. Mary's group. One of that group, Achille Cattanei, the little major, died in 1952. Captain Leonida Gorlato became a judge and, though not himself an artist, lived for a time in a state-provided apartment in Titian's house in Pieve di Cadore; Gambetti visited him there. Gorlato died in 1981.

Gambetti and his wife, Luisa, a small and intense woman with dark hair and green eyes, lived in an apartment and studio high above the Porto Vecchio in Genoa, overlooking rooftop apartments with potted flowers and lemon trees. Though he had heart trouble, Gambetti continued to paint professionally until near his death in 1988.

During the Hereford days, Mario de Cristofaro told Franco Di Bello he did not expect to live long, probably not past thirty-five or forty. He did not know why—he just felt it. Di Bello saw him only twice after repatriation. His friend died of leukemia in 1964, when he was fifty. One of his other predictions was that he would never marry; but he did so, in the mid–1950s, and his widow, Clara, and two sons survive.

Giuseppe Berto died of cancer in 1978. His first published novel, *Il cielo è rosso,* written at Hereford, won the Premio Firenze for literature in 1948, and his *Il male oscuro,* published in 1964, won both the Premio Viareggio and the Premio Campiello.

Aurelio Manzoni, Di Bello's roommate, is a prominent lawyer in Milan. His many activities include writing and editing for a monthly paper called *Volontà,* published specifically for a readership of non-collaborators—veterans of camps in Hawaii, Kenya,

India, South Africa, Australia, and the Middle East, as well as Hereford. One issue of the paper contained an editorial statement condemning what it said was thirty-seven years' suppression and slanting of news about the regime under which "Italy was successful in attaining prestige and in counting for something in the world." Although integrity and consistency are the motives that the *Nons* usually cite for their refusal to collaborate, this publication for *Nons* is clearly nostalgic, and fiercely so, about the Italy that entered the war against the Allies. Fascism is outlawed in Italy and seems to have about the same social status there as racism has in the United States. But of course nostalgia is no crime.

Though *Volontà* arranges reunions of *Nons*, not all *Nons* have kept in touch with others. Manzoni had not seen Di Bello for more than thirty years after 1950 and had thought him dead—a friend had passed along a report to that effect. Di Bello had not seen Gambetti since the war; had not known whether he was alive.

Di Bello has expressed great respect and liking for these men. But although he was an unhesitating *Non* and still has no reservations about that position, Di Bello is not pleased with the current attitudes of all who agreed with him. He deplores postures "which tend to defend themselves at any cost and, consequently, to charge all the faults on the opponent whoever he might be." He despises some people's "tendency to show themselves as poor martyrs who have suffered because the rest of the world is mean." These aversions seem at home with the habits of analysis and self-assessment taught by Coach Mario Cabbai and by Ida di Bello. As for the state of mind which, even after the St. Mary's project, caused Di Bello to write *"Addio America Amara,"* that has radically changed. Di Bello is a strong friend of the United States and would love to live there, especially in the California coastal area between Monterey and Santa Barbara. His wife, Ines, though, like Evelyn Coyle, feels bound by family ties to the city where they live—Pordenone, thirty miles west of Udine at the base of the craggy *Prealpi Venete.*

Di Bello's attachment to the United States is partly political. One thing he is immoderate about is communism, and his opposition goes back many years. During his Hereford days, he hoped that Germany would win the war—but only, he says, because one of the Allies was the Soviet Union. This alliance he could not understand. In the context of his antipathy he expressed himself in a letter on the subject of *Non*s who still hate America:

> It's beyond me, indeed, to understand how can people—after what we've seen in the last 40 years, slaughter of million people here and there in the world, million people who lost their life to escape communist persecution, only 8.000 Italian prisoners of war in Russia come back to Italy out of 80.000 (and never we had news about the other 72.000), thousands of people still completely deprived of liberty and kept in lagers or madhouses, dead and disaster all over this dirty world—how can people, I said, remain so rigid and intransigent about minor matters and fact occurred 38/39 years ago and anyway exsagerated, since it is proved that nobody died because of them.

Di Bello had gone back to Udine after the war disillusioned and uninterested in continuing his military career. He was sick over the chaos in Italy. The greeting by peddlers in boats outside Naples had permanently embittered him. "I began to hate my people from that moment," he said. He spent six months with his family, recovering his balance.

The Germans, he found, had not left a good impression in Udine during the occupation; the people looked upon the present Allied occupying troops as liberators. Food had been short during the occupation (for the German troops, too), though there was plenty by the time Di Bello returned. His mother, who had taught at Pradamano until 1945, would buy produce and meats from farmers and orchardists in the village, where she had dozens of former pupils. She brought food home on her bicycle, a dangerous thing to do. For young men like Bruno di Bello, just going out on the streets was risky: the Germans had press gangs out. To evade them, Bruno hid in the cellar or the attic of the di Bello apartment and, often, went to Padua, where he was a student in the university (Padua was under the Salò government, whereas the Germans considered Udine their own). Eventually he found out that somebody had tipped off the Germans to his presence and that he was on a list of those to be arrested the next day. But the German commandant's secretary, a pretty redhead of about thirty, lived below the di Bellos; and she had a crush on Bruno. She warned him and for many days hid him in her own room.

(When the di Bellos got their first word about Franco after his capture they rejoiced to know he was safe, and his father was specifically happy to learn that his custodians were Americans, who he was sure would treat him relatively well. The news came in a radio broadcast from London, which was forbidden listening.)

Since he was not going back into the army, Di Bello decided to make use of his ability to draw. He entered the Istituto Universitario di Architettura in Venice, bought books, and started studying for the November examinations. But at the beginning of October, he went to Brescia to visit a friend. In a street there, he heard martial music approaching from the distance, and soon a *bersaglieri* company came around the corner on the double. "I found that something was still worthy," Di Bello said. Two days later he applied for re-entry into the army. He was called up on October 28, sent to the *bersaglieri* unit in Brescia, and immediately made a captain.

His battalion was moved to Pordenone in August 1949, and after a year he was given his own company. Along with the colonel in command of the unit, he went to a fabric shop in Pordenone to buy curtains for the officers' barracks. There he met the shopkeeper's daughter, a quietly radiant girl named Ines Durat. They were married in October 1951.

In 1959, a major now, Di Bello was chosen to attend the Command and General Staff College at Fort Leavenworth, Kansas. He left, alone, in June, and ten days after his arrival got word that his father had died.

Ines joined him in Kansas that fall. Before Christmas, they drove to Dawn, Texas, to pay a surprise visit to Paul Artho, who had become Di Bello's close friend during the project at St. Mary's. Neighbors told them how to find the place, and in the old adobe house they were greeted by Paul's daughter, Grace.

"I would like to see Paul," Di Bello said.

"Who are you?" Grace asked.

"Listen, I would like to make him a surprise," Di Bello said.

Artho had just finished a nap. He came in, wearing overalls and a hat, a little irritated and suspicious. "Good morning, Paul Artho," Di Bello said. "Do you know me?" He did not. Di Bello said he would give him a few minutes to remember him. Artho played the game, not cheerfully: had he met him on the ship to Europe in 1954? in Switzerland? in Dallas? None of those. "I'm sure you're a salesman," Artho said. He was getting angry. Finally Ines said, "Come on, stop it," and her husband identified himself.

"Frank! I didn't remember you," Artho said. He took off his hat and threw it on the floor. From the next room, he brought back the page from his pocket notebook on which, fourteen years before, Di Bello had sketched a map of Italy and written "Udine" in the northeast corner. Artho had kept it all that time. The men embraced, crying.

The Di Bellos stayed four nights at the Artho place, going to midnight mass at St. Mary's on December 24 and having dinner with George and Mary

Brockman on the day after Christmas. Di Bello took snapshots of the church and of the ruins of the checkpoint at the entrance to the former prison camp, later sending copies to John Coyle. "This is the inside of 'St. Mary,'" he wrote on the back of a picture. "As you can see, everything is perfectly the same as we left it on the 8th of December, 1945." Not quite everything was, as a matter of fact. The Reverend Andrew Marthaler, pastor of St. Mary's from 1948 to 1958, had had a drape made for the main work, the oil of the *Assumption*. The painting would be shown only on special days, on the premise, Marthaler explained in a letter, that familiarity breeds contempt *("quotidiana vilescunt")*. When the drape is open, it forms a soft border across the top of the painting, and Marthaler thought this an appropriately feminine touch. Di Bello thinks it is disgusting. But the drape is pulled back more often now than it was in the Marthaler days.

After the assignment in Kansas, Di Bello spent a decade in various command, teaching, and administrative posts, including, as a full colonel in 1967, the assignment he had always wanted: command of a *bersaglieri* regiment. It was the famous Eighth, at Pordenone. When that year ended, he attended NATO Defense College in Rome, toured installations in the United States and elsewhere, and after graduation was sent to Brussels, the new location of Supreme Headquarters of NATO. There, in his second year, he had an assignment that initially interested him but that turned out to be, he said, "one of the most idiot things that I have ever done."

He joined a group seeking an accord between NATO and the Warsaw Pact countries. There were studies, proposals, lectures, and meetings, "all of it in the illusion of having the Russians reduce their forces on the border of the Iron Curtain according to the reductions we [especially the United States] would have made on our part." When he left in December 1972, he said in an address to the full assembly that as a soldier he had performed his assigned duty as well as possible, but that he had never believed that the Soviets would agree to a mutual and equitable reduction of forces. If they did withdraw, he said, it would be only for a couple of hundred kilometers, whereas U.S. troops would have to cross the Atlantic. He had never seen the Soviet Union renouncing its best weapon, which was, he said, the help it received from Communists in all NATO countries, including Italy. More than half the audience applauded his speech, Di Bello said.

On his departure, he was promoted to general. That was a political rank, in his estimation. Army politics disgusted him, and so did unions through which soldiers could question orders. He therefore asked that he be put *a disposizione*—at full pay and on call but without duties, renouncing further promotions. His years in this status, all of which he spent in Pordenone, ended on September 4, 1978, when he reached the age of fifty-eight, the upper limit for brigadier generals.

And that was the quiet end of the military career that he had embraced with fervor, later upholding its ideals, as he saw them, in the face of hunger and a comparatively rigorous confinement. Is he proud to have had that career? In a way, yes. He is more than proud, he says, "of having done honestly what I was called to do." He is sure in his conscience that he did his duty according to the rules. But as for having been an officer in a country that he sees as getting worse and worse economically and politically; afflicted with crime, terror, and the Mafia; its armed forces unmotivated, undisciplined—he cannot say he is proud of having been an officer in *this*. He believes that Italy is more fragmented in its interests and goals, from one part to the other, than it was sixty-eight years ago, at the beginning of the Fascist regime.

What, then, if Mussolini should return to today's Italy? "He wouldn't even be able to begin," Di Bello said. "A guy like that would be not only tragic but ridiculous." In the early 1920s, Italy enjoyed at least the memory of having been on the winning side in World War I. There is no such memory as an influence toward unity today; the loss in World War II was "an about-face of which we are very ashamed." It was Mussolini's great mistake to imagine that a people more crafty than belligerent, a people with a history only of small provincial fights, a people lacking the warrior tradition of Germans, Vikings, ancient Romans, and Alexandrian Greeks, could ever be inspired to fight a great war greatly. So Di Bello believes.

In June 1981 Di Bello returned to Umbarger and Hereford for a visit, this time accompanied by Bruno, his brother. He saw the Brockmans again, and Harvey

and Ormalene (Brockman) Artho. He went out to see
the sculptured concrete memorial (since restored but
at the time half-ruined by vandals) that prisoners had
erected in a field during the last months of the camp.
Of course he took another look at the paintings and
carvings at St. Mary's Church. With Ormalene he
visited Jerry Skarke Gerber, whose husband had died
of a heart attack in 1978. He went to the Umbarger
cemetery and stood at the grave of Paul Artho, who
had died in 1963. There, he said, he wept "as if Paul
was a brother of mine." Harvey and Ormalene, along
with Harvey's sister and brother-in-law, returned the
visit to the Di Bellos two months later in Pordenone
and Udine. In April 1988 Di Bello once again visited
Umbarger and Hereford, and in December of that
year he and his wife were hosts to visitors from Pennsylvania: John and Evelyn Coyle. It was the first time
John and Franco had seen each other since before the
Hereford camp was closed.

Franco and Ines Di Bello, who have no children,
live in an apartment a half-block from one of the main
streets of Pordenone. Their living room walls are
covered with paintings by Italian artists, some of them
contemporary, though only three or four of Di Bello's
own are among them. Franco dropped painting in
1978 but was talking recently of taking it up again. He
spends much time reading astronomy and military history. Though he looked pudgy in a snapshot taken
during his 1959 trip to Umbarger, he eats sparingly
now and looks trim. In the evenings, the Di Bellos

spend hours watching televised variety programs and serials, most of them American with dubbed-in Italian.

His experience in the prison camp, Di Bello says, changed him; the project at St. Mary's, not so much. Umbarger gave him his first chance to meet ordinary Americans, and as he became acquainted with Umbarger people he lost his bitterness against the *camans*, coming to consider them like the others except for attitudes that their position as captors required of them. (So he says; still, there was that parting entry in his journal.) But having been a prisoner, he finds, has affected him deeply. In this experience, "you learn a lot the value of freedom, the value of disposing of yourself as you like. You learn that you have more duties than rights." Submitting to the control of "people more stupid than you" and living far from your loved ones intensify both hatred and love; "in other words, you learn the taste of life." If he had not been in on the St. Mary's project, the pleasant part of his captivity would have been less, he says, "but I think that altogether I would have considered it a positive experience."

Di Bello's brother, Bruno, is a leading surgeon in Udine. He is married and has two children.

Neither of the clergymen closest to the Hereford prisoners and their hunger at the Hereford camp is still alive. The chaplain, Achilles Ferreri, apparently left the camp a little before it closed. Bishop Fitz-Simon, in a letter early in January, 1946, commended Ferreri for his work at the camp, saying he had "had to battle with many difficulties because of the attitude of the various Commanding Officers under whom he has served." And he added, "His health has broken down under the strain and he is being given a medical discharge."[1] Ferreri went back to Ohio for at least a while after leaving Hereford. He died in Cleveland in 1961. FitzSimon, the decisive force in obtaining an adequate diet for the prisoners, died on July 2, 1958. In the summer of 1949 he went to Rome, reporting afterward that he had met several of the former *herefordiani* there.

Umbarger has the same church, the same surnames, and many of the same houses that it had in 1945. There are fairly recent one-story houses along the mostly dirt streets to the north of the highway. One of them, a pleasant place with pretty trees and grass, belongs to the Brockmans. Another, only a block southeast of St. Mary's, is Jerry Skarke Gerber's home. The rectory, just north of the church, has been remodeled and enlarged. On the parking lot to the east of the church is a long white shed—the parish hall. Every year on the second Sunday of November the Fall German Sausage Festival, originated in 1952 as a fund raiser, brings hundreds of Panhandle people to the hall for sausages, sauerkraut, green beans, and homemade bread—a meal that might have been served to the prisoners at St. Mary's.

Henry Bracht, who had the machine shop that some of the prisoners used, died in 1983. His wife, Amalia, has moved to a retirement center. The Bracht cherry orchard was flourishing in the early 1980s, and Mrs. Bracht told a visitor she had made herself so tired working with the trees a few days earlier that she had gone into the house and cried. The story was reminiscent of Marie Skarke and her fence posts.

Meinrad Hollenstein, who drove for John Coyle on the rabbit-hunting trips, fell from a tree he was pruning. A fence picket pierced his chest and neck. He lived several years after that, dying of other causes in July 1959 when he was seventy-seven years old.

Mathilda, the housekeeper for Father John Krukkert, died of cancer in Amarillo on August 1, 1973, at the age of sixty-eight. Her son, John, was living in downstate Texas in the early 1980s.

Krukkert, it is said, went out on a blustery, chilly day to attend another priest's funeral and to help officiate at graveside. He had been coughing that morning; the exposure was perhaps a turning point. He had a heart attack on the afternoon of November 10, 1947, and died early the next morning in St. Anthony's Hospital in Amarillo, having lived for not quite two years after the completion of the project at St. Mary's, where he was still pastor.

Paul Artho finally made it to Switzerland; there is a photograph of him eating soup aboard ship in September 1954, wearing a checked shirt and city trousers with suspenders. In 1958 his second wife, Mary, died at the age of fifty-one. Sister Martina, the teacher, remembered a school theme by his son Kenneth telling how he had taken his mother to the doctor for a diagnosis after she became ill. All day he waited; she came out and sat in the car, saying that Papa wouldn't like this at all. They went home; Kenneth hung around to listen; finally she told his father that she had cancer. Paul wept and wept.

In 1951 Paul Artho took a train to Canada and visited a reclusive cousin named Joe Artho, whom he knew only by correspondence. He got off the train beyond White Horse in the Yukon Territory and walked perhaps twenty miles into the country. Of course he hadn't told the cousin he was coming. Joe met him with a gun. To prove his identity, Paul had to fish in his luggage for a letter that Joe had written him. Then it was all right. The next morning, Paul heard his host leave and after a while got up and scratched the soot from a window with his pocketknife to look out. Joe was headed back to the cabin from a stream, carrying a salmon as long as his arm. They ate part of it for breakfast. Another item in their diet was caribou meat. Paul stayed about a week and went back to his farm. In his vigorous curiosity he had not essentially changed from the young immigrant who rode a fine horse to Clovis or the man who stood for hours in St. Mary's Church, pumping a friendly artist for all the information he could get about life in Italy.

Paul Artho was sixty-eight when he died. Six of his seven sons were his pallbearers after the funeral at St. Mary's, and he was buried in the Umbarger cemetery alongside his two wives. To Di Bello, he had been a sensitive and intelligent friend, "a man who believed in the necessity of sacrifice and in the fact that certain people have more duties than rights, a sturdy and determined worker but also a gentle and deeply honest individual."

Harvey and Ormalene Artho live on their farm
south of Wildorado, which is eighteen or twenty miles
northwest of Umbarger. They have seven living
children; a son Ned, was killed in a football accident
in 1971.

Jerry Skarke Gerber is liturgy chairman of the
Diocesan Council of Catholic Women. She has
retained her childhood faith. When she showed the
painting in St. Mary's of the angel holding the inscription that had hung over the head of Jesus on the
cross, she said it made her angry to think of people
mocking Christ, as in the Bible. "But we are doing the
same thing today," she said—we mock Christ, that is,
with abortions, divorce, stealing, and cheating. When
you beat someone, she said, you are beating Christ, because each person is a part of Christ's body. In her
family life, Mrs. Gerber has not had an easy time of it.
In 1974 she and her husband lost a son, Dwayne, twenty-four years old, in an automobile accident. Her
husband's death followed four years later. Her
parents were eventually divorced; Otto died in 1979;
Marie lives with Jerry. The three Gerber daughters all
married Protestants, and two have had problems in
their married lives. Jerry Gerber's son, Gary, drives a
cattle truck and does custom combining in the business that he and she own.

Jerry Gerber's smile does not show her life of hard
work and sadness anymore than it did, to judge by pictures, when she was eighteen.

St. Mary's Church has a remodeled main entrance
with a portico and with a ramp for wheelchairs. The

trees have been removed from the sides, and the parking lots have been enlarged, partly to accommodate the fall festival. Otherwise it looks much the same from the outside as it did in 1945. Inside, the church has new pews and a different altar. It has the *Assumption,* often draped, and the murals and carvings from the days of the Hereford camp. But the only explicit indication of the coming-together of cultures and motives that distinguished the church forty-five years ago is on the plaque at the entrance, with its nine Italian names and its inscription telling what happened inside.

Notes

ONE

1. United States Department of the Interior, National Park Service: National Register of Historic Places Inventory—Nomination Form, items 7 and 8, undated, pp. 44-47. A letter to the Catholic Diocese of Amarillo, accompanying the form and dated 1 April 1983, is in the archives of the Catholic Diocese of Amarillo.

2. Although Franco Di Bello's letter seemed to suggest that the deaths in camp were caused by inadequate nutrition, Di Bello later told me, both in an interview (23 October 1982) and in two other letters (16 January 1982, citing the Italian Ministry of Defense; and 18 February 1983), that this was not the case. A report to the Eighth Service Command in Dallas, 16 November 1945, said four deaths had occurred in the last twenty-two months. It listed the causes as coronary thrombosis; cerebral apoplexy, secondary to hypertension; traumatic cardiac rupture— a stab wound to the heart; and neurosyphilis (cerebral accident). National Archives, Record Group 389.

3. The population of the camp varied. Counts included 1,928 on 21 July 1943 (Archives 389, document 8031502); 1,637 on 12 February 1944 (Archives, 8031503); and 2,872 on 21 July 1944, including either 261 or 361—both figures are given—at a side camp at Fort Sumner, New Mexico (Archives, 8031504). An article in the *Hereford Brand*, 24 December 1964, says 3,099 were

shipped out on troop trains in February 1946. The estimate of the number of officers is from Franco Di Bello.

THREE

1. Martha H. Byrd, "Captured by the Americans," *American History Illustrated*, February 1977, p.26; and Flavio Giovanni Conti, "Il problema politico dei prigionieri italiani nei rapporti con gli alleati (1943-1945)," *Storia contemporanea* 7, no. 4, December 1976.

2. Byrd, p. 35.

FOUR

1. Unsigned, undated note in the Joseph R. Carvolth Papers, in archives of U. S. Army Military History Institute, Carlisle, Pennsylvania.

2. Undated note, signed "Sottufficiali Democratici," in Prisoner of War Camps, WWII—Hereford, Texas, in library of U. S. Military History Institute.

3. Lieutenant Pietro Formai, report to "The American Command," 29 April 1945, in Prisoner of War Camps, library of Institute.

4. "An officer," note to Joseph R. Carvolth, 10 August 1945, in Carvolth papers.

5. General Nazzareno Scattaglia, letter to Legation of Switzerland, 13 October 1944, in Carvolth papers.

6. Captain Henry N. Duff, letter to "Commanding Officer" of camp, 16 September 1944, in Carvolth papers.

7. Byrd, p. 27, says the United States built its POW camps in isolated places for security.

FIVE

1. Armando Boscolo, *Fame in America*, 2nd ed. (Milan: Edizione La Motonautica, 1965), p. 63.

2. Giuseppe Berto, "L'inconsapevole approccio," introduction to his *Le opere di Dio* (Milan: Mondadori, 1980), p. 28. He does not name Esther Klinke.

3. The letters were supplied by Ann Payton Connelly.

4. *Hereford P. O. W. Camp, 1942-1946,* Castro County Historical Commission, 1988. Details were supplied by Franco Di Bello in an interview of 22 October 1982 and in drawings by Alfredo Rizzon, who was an Italian officer in captivity at the camp.

5. The Reverend Joseph Saraceno, letter to the Most Reverend Laurence J. FitzSimon, 21 June 1945, in Amarillo Catholic archives. Letter from FitzSimon to the Honorable Eugene Worley, 15 September 1945, in Catholic archives. In numerous interviews with former prisoners, I have always been told that food was plentiful at the camp until early in May 1945. In the archives and library of the Institute at Carlisle, I found no complaints about the food before that time. Further substantiation is in a letter to me of 16 July 1981 from Franco Di Bello and in interviews with three former civilian or military employees of the camp: Grant Hanna, 19 March 1982; Bill Phipps, on the same day; and Guy Lawrence, 12 July 1982.

SIX

1. Cited in Arnold Krammer, *Nazi Prisoners of War in America* (New York: Stein and Day, 1971), p. 240; and in Boscolo, *Fame,* p. 173 n.

2. "Anger at Nazi Atrocities Rising but U. S. Treats Prisoners Fairly," unsigned article, *Newsweek* 25, no. 19, 7 May 1945, p. 58.

3. Unsigned editorial, *Commonweal* 42, 20 March 1945, 4.

4. Cited in Judith M. Gansberg, *Stalag U. S. A.* (New York: Crowell, 1977), p. 40.

5. Police photographs in files of Joe D. Rogers, Hereford.

6. Translation of speech in Carvolth file, Institute.

7. P. Schnyder, International Red Cross Committee, report of visit of 24-25 November 1944 to the Hereford camp, in National Archives, RG 389.

8. *Texas Almanac,* 1982-83, p. 119.

9. Lieutenant Domenico Manganelli to S. Dante Manganelli, 14 July 1945, in Carvolth papers.

10. First Lieutenant Osvaldo Barilari to Ralph Scerbo, 3 September 1945, in Carvolth papers.

11. Giuseppe Berto to Tito Tognonato, 13 July 1945, in library of Institute.

SEVEN

1. Order from Colonel Joseph R. Carvolth, 16 May 1945, "Engine-Ears Grapevine," in Carvolth papers.

2. "Mostra d'arte dei prigionieri di Hereford," brochure, August 1945, in Di Bello's collection.

3. I have not been able to find the correspondence.

4. Report by War Prisoners Aid, undated, in National Archives, RG 389.

5. Achilles P. Ferreri and James Salvi to FitzSimon, 12 September 1945, in Catholic archives.

6. The Reverend D. Giacomo Sarra to FitzSimon, undated (probably late 1945), in Catholic archives.

7. *Amarillo Daily News,* 16 October 1945.

8. "Lost Battalion Leader Comes Home," Lewis T. Nordyke, *Amarillo Daily News,* 15 October 1945, p. 1.

9. Edwards Studio advertisement, *Amarillo Daily News,* 16 October 1945, p. 5.

10. "German Rations Are Cut Sharply," Associated Press article, *Amarillo Daily News,* 16 October 1945, p. 1; "Text of Eisenhower's Letter to Truman on Displaced Persons," *New York Times,* 17 October 1945, p. 8; and "Eisenhower Fears German Inflation," Anthony Leviero, *Times,* 17 October 1945, p. 9.

EIGHT

1. Obituary, *The Register,* publication of Catholic Diocese of Amarillo, 16 November 1947.

2. Personal history, undated, in Catholic archives; interview with the Right Reverend Monroe John Matthiessen, 30 September 1982; and Krukkert obituary, ibid.

3. The Most Reverend Robert E. Lucey to P. Friemel, 24 December 1937 and 22 June 1938, in Dolje file in Catholic archives; Dolje obituary in *The Register,* 23 January 1944; and Dolje history in Catholic archives.

4. FitzSimon to Dolje, 25 September 1943, in Catholic archives.

5. Photograph in *The Register,* 16 November 1947.

NINE

1. Weather statistics in *Amarillo Daily News,* 23 October 1945.

2. I have not been able to trace Sanvito and Zorzi to their homes in Italy.

3. Henry Bracht interview, 20 March 1982. John Coyle remembers nothing of this episode.

TEN

1. Noted in FitzSimon file, Catholic archives.

2. FitzSimon to Major General Richard Donovan, 13 June 1943, and Donovan to FitzSimon, 19 June 1943, in Catholic archives.

3. The Reverend Joseph Saraceno to FitzSimon, 4 June 1945, in Catholic archives.

4. Major Luigi Cabitto to General Nazzareno Scattaglia, 17 August 1945, in Carvolth papers.

5. FitzSimon to the Honorable Eugene Worley, 15 September 1945, in Catholic archives.

6. "La Guardia Eases His Meatless Days," unsigned, *New York Times,* 12 March 1945, p. 1.

7. "Fresh Meat Ration of Prisoners of War Cut by Army to Hearts, Livers, Kidneys," unsigned article, ibid., 15 April 1945, p.9.

8. Policy directive from Army Service Forces to commanders of prison camps, undated, in archives of Institute. It consists of testimony given by Brigadier General B. M. Bryan, assistant provost marshal general, before the House Committee on Military Affairs on 26 April 1945.

9. Gansberg, *Stalag,* p. 40.

10. Captain Floyd A. Spencer, inspection report of 8 October 1945, in Carvolth papers.

11. Carvolth memo, "Service Command Conference," to Commanding General, Eighth Service Command, 10 June 1945, in Carvolth papers.

12. Report of Special War Problems Division, Department of State, to General B. M. Bryan, 12 September 1944, in National Archives, RG 389.

13. The son spoke to me briefly on the telephone about his father but did not answer a letter asking for more information. In the conversation, he told me that his father's papers were in the Army Military History Institute at Carlisle, Pennsylvania. That collection has provided information of great value to this account.

14. Typewritten charts made during inspection of 28 October 1945, not otherwise identified; in Carvolth papers. Di Bello and other former POWs say the Red Cross did the weighing. Boscolo, *Fame,* p. 190, says the Red Cross made photographs of emaciated prisoners.

ELEVEN

1. Records of district clerk, Deaf Smith County, Texas.

2. Death certificate of Mrs. Paul Artho, in Deaf Smith County records.

3. Proclamation of Governor Dan Moody, 21 September 1928, granting a ninety-day extension of a previous furlough, in Texas State Archives, Austin.

THIRTEEN

1. Reports of the inspection were made by General Nazzareno Scattaglia and Lieutenant Stanley Deal. Scattaglia's report, dated 13 November 1945, was submitted to the Italian Royal Embassy; in Carvolth papers.

2. Office of Texas state climatologist, College Station, interview of 2 March 1983; and the Scattaglia report to the Italian Embassy (n. 1).

3. Dick J. Reavis, "Growing Up Gringo," *Texas Monthly* 10, no. 8, August 1982, p. 174.

4. Untitled, undated document in Carvolth file.

FOURTEEN

1. I am sure they enjoyed the experiences. Thirty-eight years later, I went with the Coyles to Palo Duro Canyon, and the three of us rented horses. It was the first time either of them had ridden. They seemed thrilled. Everything pleased and interested them—the fertile land, the occasional rural Western-style mansion, the sunshine, even the constant wind. They were ideal tourists and perfect adapters.

2. Carvolth memorandum to Eighth Service Command, 10 June 1945, in Carvolth papers.

3. National Weather Service records, Amarillo station.

SIXTEEN

1. Bryan to Worley, 23 October 1945, in Catholic archives.

2. Eighth Service Command notice to Carvolth of scheduled inspection. The notice, dated 25 October 1945, is in the Carvolth papers. Letter to me from Francoise Perret, Department of Principles and Law, International Red Cross, Geneva, Switzerland, 25 March 1983.

3. In FitzSimon file, Catholic archives.

4. FitzSimon to the Most Reverend Amleto G. Cicognani, apostolic delegate, Washington, D. C., 9 November 1945, in Catholic archives.

5. FitzSimon to Cicognani, 10 November 1945, in Catholic archives.

6. Boscolo, *Fame*, p. 191. Also, interview with Di Bello, 25 October 1982.

7. "Conversation between Captain Dawson and Lt. Colonel Stephen M. Farrand, 17 November 1945 on Italian situation," in National Archives, RG 389.

8. Captain Lyle T. Dawson, report to Colonel Joseph R. Carvolth, 19 November 1945, in Carvolth papers.

9. Brigadier General B. M. Bryan, "Memorandum for the Record," 19 November 1945, in Reports of Inspection, Hereford, Texas, in National Archives, RG 389, Box 1447.

10. Colonel A. B. Johnson, acting for the Provost Marshal General, letter to Special Projects Division, Department of State, 29 December 1945, in National Archives, RG 389, Box 1447.

11. Dawson report to Carvolth, in Carvolth papers.

12. Order from Provost Marshal General's office, via Eighth Service Command, 30 April 1945, in Carvolth papers.

13. Bryan to Worley, 4 February 1946, in Carvolth papers.

14. FitzSimon to Fiorello La Guardia, 6 December 1945, in Catholic archives.

15. Luis Hortal to Carvolth, 1 December 1945, in Carvolth papers.

16. Colonel Alexander Adair to Carvolth, 17 September 1945, in Carvolth papers.

17. Carvolth's report to Eighth Service Command, 10 June 1945, in Carvolth papers.

SEVENTEEN

1. Weather forecast, *Amarillo Daily News*, 9 December 1945, p. 1.

2. The inscription reads: "ITALICI MILITES, IN MAXIMO NOVISSIMO BELLO CAPTIVI, HOC OPUS PERFECERUNT AD DEI GLORIAM ENARRANDAM ET MEMORIA REMOTAE IN-FELICIS PATRIAE HONORANDUM."

3. U. S. Representative Paul J. Kilday to FitzSimon, 5 October 1945, citing statements made to him by Brigadier General B. M. Bryan.

4. "12,000 in 2 Camps Await Transport," *New York Times,* 28 December 1945, p. 2; "Seaman Shortage Delays 121 Ships," unsigned, *New York Times,* 30 December 1945, p. 1.

5. The Reverend James Salvi to the Most Reverend Amleto G. Cicognani, 4 January 1946; and FitzSimon to Cicognani, 3 January 1946, in Catholic archives.

6. Di Bello interview, 25 October 1982. Boscolo, *Fame,* p. 201, says fifteen guards pummeled the lieutenant with baseball bats.

7. Report in Carvolth papers.

8. Second Lieutenant Anthony S. Dolozik's report, 24 January 1946, in Carvolth papers. The friend is Giuseppe Giorgi of Pordenone.

9. Carvolth letter to Fort Bliss commander, 12 March 1946, in Carvolth papers.

10. Grant deed no. 47211, records of Orange County, California.

EPILOGUE

1. FitzSimon to Amleto G. Cicognani, 3 January 1946, in Catholic archives.

Bibliography

Unpublished Documents:

Files on John Krukkert, Laurence J. FitzSimon, and John J. Dolje. In archives of the Catholic Diocese of Amarillo.

Joseph R. Carvolth Papers. In archives of U. S. Military History Institute, Carlisle Barracks, Pennsylvania.

Modern Military Branch, National Archives. Record Group 389. Records of the Office of the Provost Marshal General, 1941—.

Prisoner of War Camps, WWII—Hereford, Texas. In library of the U. S. Military History Institute, Carlisle Barracks, Pennsylvania.

Records of the District Clerk, Deaf Smith County, Texas.

Records of Orange County, California, 1945.

Proclamation by Governor Dan Moody, September 21, 1927. In Texas State Archives, Austin.

Published Works:

Berto, Giuseppe. *Le opere di Dio.* Milan: Mondadori, 1980.

Boscolo, Armando. *Fame in America,* 2nd ed. Milan: Edizione La Motonautica, 1965.

Byrd, Martha H. "Captured by the Americans." *American History Illustrated,* February 1977, pp. 23-35.

Conti, Flavio Giovanni. "Il problema politico dei prigioneri di guerra italiani nei rapporti con gli alleati." *Storia contemporanea* VII, no. 4, December 1976.

Gansberg, Judith M. *Stalag: U. S. A.* New York: Crowell, 1977.

Hereford P. O. W. Camp, 1942-1946. Dimmitt: Castro County Historical Commission, 1988.

Krammer, Arnold. *Nazi Prisoners of War in America.* New York: Stein and Day, 1971.

Glossary of Terms

a disposizione   on disposition

A noi   to us

allievi   students

Ascolta   listen

Balilla   fascist youth group

Balilla marinaretto   "little sailor" member of Balilla

Basta   enough

belle gambe   pretty legs

bersaglieri   crack troops

Bravi   shouts of "hooray," "well done"

Buon giorno   good day

calcio   soccer

caman   POWs' word for American guard

carta da spolvero   artists' paper like brown butcher paper

Casa de las Flores   flower house (Spanish)

Dove sta Za Za   Where is Za Za

È passata la guerra   the war is over

Eh, bambino   Hey, baby

Fame   hunger

festa del fiore   flower festival

Figli della lupa   sons of the she-wolf

herefordiani   prisoners at Hereford

Il cielo è rosso   The Sky Is Red

Il Duce   the leader, Mussolini

Il male oscuro   the dark evil

Il problema politico dei prigionieri di guerra italiani nei rapporti con gli alleati   The political question of Italian prisoners of war in their relationship to the Allies

Il seme tra le spine   The Seed Amid the Thorns

il signor maestro   the teacher

IL'inconsapevole approccio   The Unwitting Approach

la fame   the hunger

Lacchè   lackey

La Vispa Teresa   Happy Teresa

Le opere di Dio   The Works of God

Lei   you (polite form)

Lustrascarpe   shoe-shiner

Mamma mia   my goodness

Marcia Reale   royal hymn

Nons   Italian POWs who refused to collaborate

O mia bela madunina   a song title in dialect

O salutaris   a Latin benedictory hymn

paesà   countryman (dialect)

Porcamadonna   pig-madonna

Prealpi Venete   a range of Alpine foothills

Premio Campiello   a literary prize

Premio Viareggio   a literary prize

Quando va arrivato in dentro li Italia, no dimenticar to scrivere to le donna   when you get back to Italy, don't forget to write to the lady (Coyle's admonition)

Scuola Militare   a military academy

Servo   servant

Sottufficiali Democratici   democratic noncoms

Storia contemporanea   contemporary history

tagliatelle   a kind of pasta

Tantum ergo   a Latin benedictory hymn

Tu   you (familiar form)

Vangelo   the Gospels

Viva il Re   long live the king

Volontà   Will

Vous allez   you go (French)

zusammen mar[s]chi[e]ren   march together (German)